YORKSHIRE'S ROOTS

a Pre-Conquest Amble through the Past

Howard M. Beck

A Power is passing from the earth
To breathless Nature's dark abyss;
But when the great and good depart
What is it more than this—

—Wm. Wordsworth

Published by Sigma Leisure – an imprint of
Sigma Press, 1 South Oak Lane, Wilmslow, Cheshire SK9 6AR, England.

British Library Cataloguing in Publication Data
A CIP record for this book is available from the British Library.

ISBN: 1-85058-490-7

Typesetting and Design by: Sigma Press, Wilmslow, Cheshire.

Printed by: MFP Design & Print

Cover illustration: Ingleborough Hill, site of an Iron Age hillfort, possibly the Rigodunum mentioned by Ptolemy.

Maps, illustrations and photographs: by the author, except where noted.

Preface

This book tells the long and colourful history of Yorkshire, from its mist-shrouded beginnings in the early Stone Age up to the arrival of the Normans under Duke William of Normandy. From then onwards, English history is well documented and therefore 1066, a momentous date for the newly united country, is used as a timely cut-off point.

Yorkshire is so diverse, so rich in historical sites, that it could be compared to a child's kaleidoscope in which each variation in pattern represents its own legacy of human endeavour. Important historical remains exist everywhere, simply awaiting 'discovery' by those with a will to learn and the ability, when they look, to also 'see'.

We see how, in the Dark Ages the roots of the county are irrevocably entwined with those of Northumbria; that after six centuries of sectarian strife, royal dynastic feuding, warfare, treachery and murder, each successive wave of invaders left their mark on the countryside. Each added distinctive language components that survive today in the place-names and dialect of rural hill-farming communities.

Throughout the text, historic sites and remains are described and examined from each period of the county's past and, where documentary evidence allows, its main characters are brought to life in glowing detail. Those historic sites that are mentioned are given a six-figure national grid reference to help in their location.

Where artifacts have been found or unearthed through excavation, attention is drawn to museums in which these may be seen on display. The book ends with suggestions for further reading and is supplemented by appendices which list major sites of historical importance together with their map locations for ease of reference. Guidelines are provided and useful information given on the use of the compass, map reading and plotting grid references.

At a time when traditions and time-honoured ways of life are continually being eroded, and valuable clues to the past bulldozed by the remorseless advance of what we misguidedly call 'progress', many people seek refuge and a tenuous security down memory lane. This statement is vindicated by the renaissance in rediscovered cottage crafts and changing attitudes towards architecture, all of which seem, eventually, to go full circle.

Moreover, many of us at some point in our lives have indulged in the urge to collect curios, artifacts and objets d'art that remind us of the 'good old days'. If these sentiments were not shared by the majority, then there would be little point in having museums and stately homes, no reason to preserve ancient monuments and historic sites, and the ubiquitous antique dealer would probably be on the endangered species list.

That there has always been a sense of belonging amongst Yorkshire folk goes without saying, yet if the annual turnover of visitors to the county's many museums is any measure, there would seem to be a deep-seated desire for knowledge of our colourful and fascinating past. Of the museums housing collections from the county's past, the Jorvik Centre and Yorkshire Museum in York, the Malton Museum and the Hull and East Riding Museum are especially recommended.

Of course, history is all about us, even on the very 'doorstep', and is not necessarily confined to these shrines to the past, where often we may find exhibits that distort our perspective. To emphasise this point, the visitor to a museum could be compared to an observer peering at a complex Roman floor mosaic through a pair of high-powered binoculars. The work of art may be viewed in fine detail but, due to the magnification, only a small portion of the floor is seen in each gaze. Unable to view the floor in its entirety would, under these circumstances, detract from the overall beauty and prevent the observer from appreciating it within its true context. Neither is it always possible to examine artifacts within the context in which they were used. The elaborate mosaics preserved at Aldborough, for example, stand bereft of the structure in which originally they formed the floor.

To say that history is omni-present is a real enough statement of fact, but this is not to say that it will be all that obvious. On the contrary: clues to the past often go unnoticed simply because they have been eclipsed by a 20th-century veneer. Many of us travel to work in without the slightest regard for our surroundings. Going about their automatic daily routines, the hurrying businessman or bargain-hunting housewife in the city seems oblivious even to the place names staring boldly from every street corner. For some reason, they escape curiosity, yet they can provide valuable information about our ancestors, the lifestyle they followed and even of the landscapes in which they existed.

It could be said that the difference between the past and the future is that the former will always be there to be studied and enjoyed by anyone with a yearning for historical facts, but the latter will outlive us all. Sadly, it is all too easy to accept the uncertainty of the future at the expense of the past, yet by saving for posterity the little that has been bequeathed us, and aided by a fertile imagination and an enquiring mind, perhaps our children and their children in turn, will have their lives enriched by a deeper understanding of the county's roots. Through this means, they will be better prepared with which to come to terms with history in the making.

The list of historical remains is almost endless, and many a family weekend or day trip into the country may be enhanced with a search for tumuli, early settlements or walking the courses of Roman roads. Scattered about the weather-scarred northern landscape, the tattered reminders of people half-forgotten, and cultures barely comprehended, lie like lonely galaxies in the vastness of a lost universe. Stone circles, megaliths and barrows, the sad skeletons of once-proud fortresses, sacred wells and evocative rock carvings seem like withered leaves blowing in an autumn breeze; each forms a chapter in the mysterious book of life's aspirations.

This is not intended as a reference book, nor is it a comprehensive treatise on any of the subjects dealt with. From the outset, the work is intended purely to increase the awareness of the interested layman, to whet the appetite of the amateur archaeologist and to engender an appreciation for a diverse heritage. This is to be found etched into the living landscape, and manifest in the folklore and traditions of a warm and friendly people, whose beginnings are rooted firmly in the distant Iron Age and beyond. If I succeed in this aim I shall be more than pleased.

Howard Beck

Acknowledgements:

I am extremely grateful for the assistance given by many individuals and organisations, all of whom have been more than generous with information and advice when most needed. Without their help this book would have been so much more difficult to produce.

I am pleased to thank Guy de la Bedoyere, Dr Julian D. Richards of the Department of Archaeology, University of York, Donald Haigh (Roman Roads Coordinator), Susan Leadbeater (Librarian) and Peter Wilson (Secretary) of the Roman Antiquities section of the Yorkshire Archaeological Society, Mr R. Cartwright of the North York Moors National Park, Michael Boardman of Humberside County Council, Bill Mitchell, former editor of *The Dalesman* and Anne Bailey (custodian) of the Roman Museum, Aldborough. I am also grateful for the warm welcome and assistance provided by the staff of the Richmondshire Museum, the Manor House Museum, Ilkley, Cliff Castle Museum, Keighley and Craven Museum, Skipton.

A special thanks is extended to Sonia Lawson for permission to use her drawing of the Burning Bartle custom, and also to Patricia Lawton and Mr John G. Hurst of the Medieval Village Research Group for the map of Wharram Percy and tales of 'lost' Yorkshire villages.

Author's Note

I have endeavoured to be as complete and thorough as is possible in dealing with historic sites, the remains of early settlements, etc, however their inclusion in the text is in no way any guarantee that a right of public access exists, nor is one implied. It should be noted also, that it is illegal to use metal detectors on private land without the express permission of the landowner, and indeed at *any time* on sites scheduled as Ancient Monuments.

Many of the maps and drawings reproduced in this book have been reproduced from aerial photograph interpretation, ground observation, or a combination of the two. Although the study of prehistoric sites through crop mark analysis is briefly discussed in the third chapter, the technique will be beyond the scope of most readers. For this reason, most sites mentioned are confined to those where there are worthwhile remains to be seen from ground observation.

To arrive at a more or less correct chronology for the events referred to in the following pages, I have mostly used as my bible the excellent works of Blair, Fletcher and the late Dr Raistrick, to whom I have to admit my debt.

Contents

Appendices

1

The Dawn of Civilization

From little spark may burst a mighty flame
– Dante.

During a period lasting from about seventy million to two million years ago, known as the Tertiary Era, the forces of Nature were still very much at work, shaping the world and moulding the land into a form approximating that which we see today. The primary mountain ranges of Europe were still being folded and uplifted, in Mid-Tertiary times, to form the Alps, the Appenines and the Pyrenees. Here in Britain the chains of hills and modest mountains were, to a degree, being fashioned by the small subsidiary ripples that were incidental to the tectonic forces at work elsewhere.

It was toward the latter end of the Tertiary Era, that many of Yorkshire's embryo rivers began cutting down their associated valleys as land drainage achieved a level of maturity. It was then that valleys took on the 'V' cross-section that is typical of a river-worn channel. Classic examples of river valleys may be seen in the Yorkshire Dales National Park at Penyghent Gill (SD862738), a deeply-incised tributary of Littondale, and in Clapdale (SD752705) north of the village of Clapham. These dales, and the Walden valley too, are features proved to have been formed by post-glacial meltwater streams.

At about this time, the climate in Britain was gradually cooling down in readiness for the final modification to the landscape. This was to be the last chapter in the preparations for the arrival of man, the great Ice Age of the Pleistocene Period, the ultimate geological event in the long history of earth's creation. It began about two million years ago and lasted until around 10,000 BC.[1]

Contrary to popular misconception, the Ice Age that followed was far from being a simple, uncomplicated episode, but instead was a cycle of glacial advances punctuated by interglacial periods of retreat relating directly to milder conditions prevailing throughout the northern hemisphere. Looking at the effect these fluctuations had on the landscape of the county, we find by far the most dramatic has been the widespread scouring or smoothing-off of the high country, particularly along that range of hills down the western side of Yorkshire known as the Pennines.

Each stage of glaciation was created by the accumulation of vast snow deposits which built up over northern Scandinavia as the climate deteriorated in the northern hemisphere. These snow fields amalgamated to form an ice cap having its hub centred upon Norway and with a secondary focal point over the outliers of Scotland. As the snow fields increased in depth so too did the pressure, with the resulting glaciers commencing a southern movement.

A feature of these ice movements was the moraines. As the glaciers inexorably advanced, material literally ground from the underlying rock was jettisoned along the glacier's flanks as a lateral moraine. As milder weather melted the ice so the 'snout' of the glacier retreated, with the result that material being pushed in front was left behind, deposited in what is termed a terminal moraine. These morainic deposits consisted of an assortment of pebbles and boulders contained in a matrix of heavy, blue-grey clay. As we shall see shortly, these moraines were to have a profound influence upon the migrations of the first people to arrive in Yorkshire.

Studies of the closing stages of the last glaciation show that in the Vale of York a chaotic state of affairs resulted from the combined effects of the coastal ice sheet and the Vale of York glacier. Normal drainage channels were disrupted, lakes were formed and drained again, boulder clays were deposited and shifted. Rivers meandered about, unable to establish a permanent course.

---

[1]
The Ice-Age in Yorkshire and Humberside.

Plate 1: The Vale of York viewed from Sutton Bank. The poorly-drained plains posed a communication problem for the Mesolithic nomad.

Exploring the Vale of York today, we can see the evidence of two great ridges of glacial drift, each about 170 feet in height and quite clearly representing the retreat points of the Vale of York glacier. One moraine passes close by the village of Escrick, about six miles south of York, and another is deposited where York itself stands. Geologists in recent years have come to accept the Escrick moraine as the southern-most limit of the last glaciation in North Yorkshire (see Fig. 1).

*   *   *

About 12,000 BC, an improvement in the climate resulted in the arrival of the first plant species, represented by the dwarf birch, which achieved a tenuous footing in the north of the region. By 7500 BC pines and juniper had joined the ranks and a steady colonisation by the plants had begun. On higher ground the dominant species were ling, crowberry and cotton grass. The climate warmed further encouraging alder, oak and hazel and the spread of heath woodlands began.

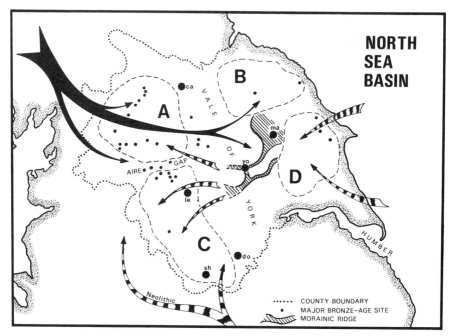

Fig. 1: Map indicating post-glacial moraines and pre-historic migration routes. Hatched arrows indicate movements of Mesolithic and Neolithic people, the solid arrows that of the Bronze Age: A) Northern Pennines; B) North York Moors; C) South Pennines; D) Yorkshire Wolds; ca) Catterick; ma) Malton; yo) York; le) Leeds; do) Doncaster; sh) Sheffield.

It was at about this time that man took his first tentative steps in Yorkshire. These people belonged to a period intermediate to the Old (Palaeolithic) and New (Neolithic) Stone Age, and which is generally referred to as the Middle (Mesolithic) Stone Age. Archaeological evidence shows that these early people were a nomadic race after the Azilians, whose remains were first identified in the caves of Mas d'Azil in France.

The Mesolithic settlers gained a foothold first of all in the region of the Yorkshire Wolds, subsisting by hunting in the virgin woodlands and fishing the many lakes and tarns left behind by the retreat of the northern ice. At this time most of the valley floors consisted of swampy scrubland, a condition that prevailed until medieval times. Looking about the county there is widespread evidence for remnant glacial lakes. Malham Tarn (SD895665) and Semerwater (SD920870) are two classic examples, while Hornsea Mere (TA190475) is probably another.

At the opposite side of the Pennines, Kingsdale at the western fringe of the Yorkshire Dales provides clues to the existence of another lake. At the bottom end of the dale can still be seen (SD695755) the remains of the moraine, known as the Raven Ray Barrier, where this was breached by Kingsdale Beck in post-glacial times. Pot-holers have in recent years explored a cave system in this valley which has demonstrated that a higher saturation level once existed as a result of the dam created by the bank of drift.

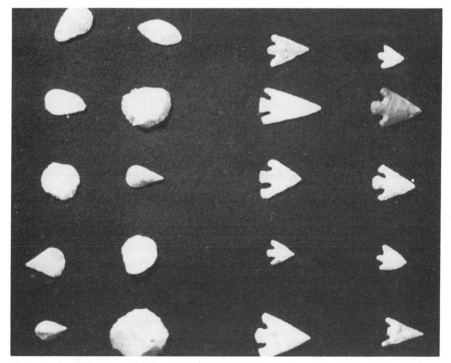

Plate 2: A collection of flint arrowheads, awls and scrapers found at various locations in Wharfedale. *(Courtesy: Donald Mellor)*

Other glacial lakes no doubt existed in Mesolithic times at Hal-steads (SD845636) at the foot of Attermire Scar just east of Settle, and at the site of the former Giggleswick Tarn (SD807648), where the excavation many years ago of an early British canoe was evidence of early man's activities in this area.

Although these Mesolithic people left few clues to their where-abouts in Yorkshire (and these confined mainly to weapons and tools) the imaginative rambler or amateur archaeologist abroad between Settle and Malham will find at Attermire Scar a feeling for those primitive hunters taking shelter in the caves that exist here. The name Attermire is commonly thought to be a corruption of Otter's Mere. If one stands in the entrance rift of the cave that looks south from this prominent limestone face, across the boggy region of Halsteads, it takes little stretch of imagination to visualize these early folk sat around a fire surveying the lake which probably once occupied this spot. Moreover, bone harpoons of Mesolithic age have been un-earthed in Attermire Cave (SD842642), and at Victoria Cave (SD839650), half a mile to the north.

Other fine harpoons have been found at Calf Hole Cave (SD964645) near Skyrethorns seven miles east, and at Star Carr (TA029812) near Scarborough, one of the first 'camping' sites to be identified with the Mesolithic culture. Yet another harpoon was dredged from the bed of the North Sea many miles off-shore, suggestive of a migratory path across what at that time was still a land bridge, albeit a region made treacherous by swamps, lagoons and capricious post-glacial drainage channels.

It would seem likely following their arrival in the eastern parts of the county, that these nomadic hunters migrated west into the York-shire Dales and south into the Pennines via the moraines at York and Escrick. These ridges of boulder clay would have provided a very convenient safe passage across an area that was still poorly drained, not unlike the Norfolk Broads or the fens of East Anglia today. Continued rising of sea levels due to a more rapid melting of the northern ice caps merely exacerbated the problems of travel through the region.

That the Mesolithic people overcame these difficulties in the Vale of York swamplands, we know from the widespread distribution of their crude tools, found throughout the county. Apart from the antler harpoon blades already mentioned, the most commonly found artifacts left behind by these people are the microliths. Often referred to as 'pygmy' flints because of their tiny dimensions, these would have been used as scrapers, boring tools and arrow tips. Over the years flint arrow heads and flakes have turned up in their thousands in the regions where Mesolithic man is known to have been active. Quite often they have made their way to the surface as a result of the subterranean activities of the mole population, turning the flints out in their hillocks to be found by walkers. The region around Lea Green (SD996633) and High Close (SE005655), north-west of Grassington, and all along the terraces flanking this dale are especially good places for picking up flints, including the occasional arrow head.

Although these people had occupied a number of cave sites along the southern fringes of the Yorkshire Dales, further to the south where caves are lacking, and around the North York Moors region, their tools and flint artifacts have been unearthed at a number of localities, usually at altitudes in excess of 800 feet. These remains are always to be found where the ground is of a sandy nature and well-drained, and the fact that charcoal of oak or birch is usually associated with them is suggestive of settlements with a history of occupation.

In the South Pennines, the vast quantities of implements, found in juxtaposition with a great many flint chips and pieces, lead archaeologists to the conclusion that some if not all of these sites were flint processing 'factories'. Additional weight is given to this idea by the discovery also, of certain materials like chert and haematite, found only in more northerly counties like Cumbria. Is it possible that Mesolithic man was already trading in flint long before the arrival of the Neolithic culture usually credited with being the first to carry out this business?

Of the more significant Yorkshire sites identified with the Mesolithic culture, there are six in the Huddersfield area, where the quantity and variety of flints discovered suggests a production process at these places. At Windy Hill (SD976142) some 5300 flints have been unearthed, while White Hill (SD991132) has yielded a further 1200. March Hill (SE008131) produced tools numbering 500, as well as 600 flint pieces, and large finds were also made at Warcock Hill

(SE074122) near Marsden, Dean Clough (SE085068) and at Cupwith Hill (SE032141). South of Huddersfield 'pygmy' flints have turned up scattered about the moors between 1000 and 1500 feet above sea level. The more important discoveries were made west of Penistone, at Wincobank (SK378910) between Sheffield and Rotherham, as well as at Stanedge (SK248845), Langsett Moors (SK160995) and at Derwent Edge (SK196890).

In the north-east of the county, around Cleveland and the North York Moors, a number of Mesolithic campsites have been identified from the flint scrapers, angle-gravers and other tools found. Apart from Star Carr which yielded harpoon blades, quantities of stone or flint utensils have been unearthed elsewhere in the region. At Cock Head (NZ727018) in Glaisdale for instance, a finely made hard stone axe head was found. Additionally flints have been found near Seamer, four miles south-west of Scarborough, and at a second site (NZ485096). Two other campsites (at NZ703106 and NZ640025) are of equal importance to that of Star Carr and have both yielded a wealth of flint remains.

*   *   *

In the West Yorkshire Pennines, the high whaleback of heather moorland forming the watershed between the valleys of the Aire and the Wharfe, and known as Rombald's Moor, has recently been recognized as an important site of prehistoric upland settlement. Archaeologists believe that the region represents a record of almost continuous occupation spanning the period between about 3,000 BC and 1,000 BC. Evidence also suggests that bands of hunter-gatherers were probably active on the moor as early as 5000 BC. This would indicate that Mesolithic nomads were hunting in the alder and hazel woodlands; the analysis of pollen from peat deposits prove that these were indigenous to the moor at that time. Certainly a number of microliths consistent with the Mesolithic culture have been discovered at a few localities in the area.

For the amateur archaeologist searching for evidence of these very early migrants, the flint and other remains are somewhat of a disappointment. As we have seen, irrespective of the obvious significance of those campsites positively connected with these hunters, we find no human remains, or clothing, nor pottery, and nothing indicating a sacred purpose.

The inhabitants of Star Carr probably roamed freely about the moorlands surrounding their camp, and it may be that there were many other occupation sites around the margins of Lake Pickering and other glacially derived meres, as well as on the higher ground of the Wolds and North York Moors. If we study the cultures which followed in the wake of the Mesolithic, we see that the technological advances introduced by these settlers directly resulted in the upland regions becoming more densely populated. For this very reason, much of the archaeological evidence of the earlier culture they displaced would have been erased and lost for all time.

No one can really be sure exactly when Mesolithic man ceased hunting the heath woodlands or gave up fishing in the lakes and tarns, but his was a harsh and uncompromising existence soon to be radically changed by a new race who arrived in the wake of more beneficial weather. It is possible, indeed highly probable, that the people of the Mesolithic were not really ousted from their lands, but rather were absorbed by the new culture thus forming a homogenous peasant population. We may never find the answer.

Just as Palaeolithic man outside our region had followed a survival pattern unchanged for millennia, so too had the folk of the Middle Stone Age carried on a similar tradition of fishing, hunting and gathering wherever the environment allowed. But as with his predecessor the livelihood of Mesolithic man was nevertheless still governed by the changing seasons. As game herds moved northwards with the warmer months of the year, likewise man the hunter travelled with them, until in Britain he eventually reached what today is Yorkshire.

He would make temporary camps or, where they existed, take shelter in caverns in the limestone country. As deteriorating weather heralded the approach of winter, both hunter and hunted would then move to lower latitudes again. In the following chapter we shall see how the arrival of the Neolithic brought with it changes that were to have far-reaching implications for early man, giving him unprecedented control over his environment and truly representing the dawning of civilization.

2

The Stone Age Time Machine

Rock ribbed and ancient as the sun.
– Bryant.

The Neolithic or New Stone Age ushered in a revolutionary way of life in which hunting, though still significant, was rapidly becoming secondary to a more organised existence characterised by the cultivation of specific wild grains and animal husbandry. Though there is still some uncertainty regarding the precise timing of the domestication of plants and animals, it would seem that it had its beginnings circa 10,000 BC in what is known as the Fertile Crescent. This is the belt of land running from the Nile in North Africa, across Israel, Syria, the southern region of Turkey and down into what was known as Mesopotamia, along the valleys of the Tigris and Euphrates rivers.

It was not until about 4,300 BC that these methods of agriculture arrived in Yorkshire with the Neolithic hunter-farmers. They subsequently absorbed the existing Mesolithic culture, forming the very first truly permanent population. They continued using stone and flint tools, but some took on a more refined form. Polished hard stone axes, referred to as *Celts*, were used, and later a trade in these was established on a nationwide basis with the 'roughs' being won from three important 'factories'. A well known site is that in the Langdale Pikes (NY275073) in the Lake District.

Some axe heads were still fashioned in the Palaeolithic tradition however, made from a grey-brown flint found in the chalk cliffs of the east coast, but being polished to a smooth finish. One such axe was found, alongside a great many 'pygmy' flints belonging to the Mesolithic, at Great Close Mire (SD907665), a little to the east of

Malham Tarn in the Yorkshire Dales. This flat marshy area, amounting to three-quarters of a square mile in extent, was probably a tarn like its neighbour immediately following the retreat of the Ice Age.

There can be little room for doubt that the reason why some tools were worked to a more refined finish during Neolithic times, may be directly attributed to the more sedentary lifestyle that came with the introduction of mixed farming. The people were released from the need to follow a nomadic way of life, migrating with the herds of game; they could put down their roots. The invention of the means to provide an infinitely more reliable food supply, would have removed much of the uncertainty of survival within the rugged Pennine regions and moorlands. Moreover, this transition from a predominantly hunting culture to one in which man was to a degree in control of his destiny, allowed more time for leisure and brought the whole community greater security and new found prosperity. These factors we find reflected in the variety of artifacts belonging to this period.

Neolithic settlers would have found valley bottoms composed of swampy scrubland dominated by willow. The higher ground where he chose to site his first settlements would however have had a dense covering of mixed deciduous forests, comprising oak, alder, yew, and lime. We know from his remains that Neolithic woman, or man, had a knowledge of sewing and basic textiles, and for this reason we can assume his camps to have been composed of hides sewn together to form tents set upon stone foundations in forest clearings. Large trees would have been burnt down after first being ring-barked to kill them, while thinner growth could be cleared using flint or stone adzes sharpened by laboriously rubbing them with other stones. The plough was not yet available, so the womenfolk may have tilled the soil using antler picks before sowing cereals.

In the limestone country of Craven it is apparent that Neolithic man occupied the same caverns as his predecessors. From some of these have been found the chattels which reflect his more organised lifestyle. Many of these remains can be seen on display in the Craven Museum in Skipton.

At Elbolton Cave (SD009613), near the secluded hamlet of Thorpe in Upper Wharfedale, the seat earths here could be likened to a prehistoric time capsule. Excavation revealed the charcoal of a number of hearths as well as the remains of wild creatures that he had pursued. The domestic breeds were represented by the bones of goat, sheep, dog and highland cattle. From the remains found here archaeologists could build up a picture of what they imagined life was like in the area during the New Stone Age.

Besides the predictable flint and stone weapons, and everyday tools for working the land, many other utensils were discovered. A whistle made from the tooth of a bear may have been used for controlling his dogs. Needles fashioned from bone were also unearthed, as well as quantities of potsherds – the remains of cooking vessels. This earthenware was very rudimentary, hand moulded and probably fired by putting embers from the fire inside the pot itself. 'Pot boilers' were small pebbles that were heated in the fireplace, before being dropped into the contents of the cooking vessel to bring it to the boil. A selection of these was found both at Elbolton Cave and at Victoria Cave (SD839650) near Settle.

Further east, the North York Moors seem devoid of Neolithic settlements, although since this region was more systematically inhabited in the following Bronze Age period, any remains may have been totally obliterated. But the New Stone Age brought with it another significant development – the use of grave goods, suggesting that man was fostering a belief in life after death. This may be explained by the removal of his preoccupation with the fight merely to survive, which no doubt would have given him the ability and the time to contemplate life in a more subjective light.

The dead were interred in groups within burial mounds, otherwise known as barrows or tumuli, and a study of these can provide vital clues to the settlement distribution of this and later cultures. Taking a closer look at these tumuli we discover two types, distinct from one another and probably reflecting geographical circumstances rather than any factor of cultural or spiritual necessity. The two types are known as long barrows and chambered tumuli or passage graves.

The long barrow is often in excess of 200 feet in length and constructed principally from earth and small rocks in either a wedge or pear shape when seen in plan. The chambered tombs on the other hand, are never more than fifty feet long and are sectioned off into separate cells or chambers leading off a passage using large slabs or rocks. The whole structure is then covered with gravel or earth leaving access to the passage clear.

It would appear that the two types also differ in the manner in which the deceased were interred. In the case of the long barrow the remains of more than one person would be buried at the same time, in a sort of sub-structure of timber and sods beneath the broad end of the mound. Chambered tombs however, were revisited over a period of time to deposit the remains of the more-recently deceased.

*   *   *

Although many tumuli have been lost due to the combined effects of weather erosion, the tumuli excavators of the 19th century and deep ploughing, there are still a great number scattered about the county. The difficulties of identifying tumuli with the Neolithic or other cultures, can be extremely difficult unless they are opened. A burial tomb on Bradley Moor near Skipton is considered (Raistrick) to be Neolithic in age.

One fine example of a Neolithic chambered burial mound (SD857733) can be found in the Yorkshire Dales 1½ miles south of the summit of Penyghent Hill, and on the Ordnance Survey maps is marked as Giant's Grave. This may be viewed by taking the B6479 road out of Settle as far as the village of Stainforth, from which the road to Halton Gill in Littondale is followed for a little over five miles. The tumulus is about fifty feet in length and can be found beside the road where this dips slightly at the head-waters of Penyghent Gill.

A few slabs, the remains of individual chambers, may still be seen. Most have disappeared, robbed by dry stone wall builders or farmers looking for new gateposts. The size of Giant's Grave would suggest that it served a large and important neolithic community. On the nearby terraces of Dawson Close there are signs of some form of settlement.

East of the Yorkshire Dales, long barrows have been found at a number of localities, except in the Vale of York. Some have been identified above 800 feet on Sleights Moor (NZ856037)in lower Eskdale and at Kepwick Moor (SE485928) around 1200 feet up in the Hambleton Hills, and also around Wass and Scarborough. Some of these tumuli were large enough to be given names such as Howe Hill, Lingrow Howe and Rob Howe.[2] The Wolds region appears to have been an important centre for the Neolithic culture, since around a dozen mounds have been found here at altitudes usually above 500 feet.

Elsewhere in the county we find further evidence of the extent of Neolithic settlement. One of the more obvious sites is at Castle Hill (SE152141) at Almondbury near Huddersfield. Although not quite 1000 feet in height, this prominent hill dominates the aspect of the South Yorkshire Pennines for miles around, and it is probably for this very reason that it had been chosen as a site for settlement and fortification by many waves of invaders.

Castle Hill, surmounted by Jubilee Tower, which was opened in 1899 to celebrate Queen Victoria's Diamond Jubilee, once commanded large gatherings as the venue for prize fighting, cock fights and dog fighting. It is shrouded in mystery and steeped in myth and legend. On the wind-swept summit a warning beacon was lit at the time of the Spanish Armada and there is even an eighty-feet deep well dating from the 14th century.

It is hardly surprising that the hill has had such a chequered past considering its strategic position and the importance of this to invaders who reached these parts. The Normans maintained a garrison here between 1147 and 1260, and no doubt the hill did not escape the attention of the Romans since their Celtic adversaries also held a fort here from the 1st century onwards.

However to really appreciate the antiquity of Castle Hill, the reader must cast his mind back some 4000 years or so, whilst standing near the Neolithic earthworks with the cold northern wind in his hair. By virtue of the earthen ditches and bankings, and the almost impregnable situation of Castle Hill, it will be at once obvious why the site was selected.

Another important location in the county that has yielded artifacts of the period is Semerwater (SD920870) near Hawes in Wensleydale.

2
   Howe comes from a Danish word for a low hill. Others such as Willy Howe
   (TA062724) in The Wolds, have long had legendary associations with the
   hobgoblins of local folklore.

Here the excavation of what proved to be an Iron Age settlement on the site of an earlier Bronze Age camp, also produced a number of flint arrow heads of Neolithic vintage. And on Rombalds Moor above Ilkley, it seems possible that Neolithic man hunted and farmed, although the intensive agriculture and encampments of the following Bronze Age have again destroyed what evidence there might have been.

*   *   *

There are some who believe that long barrows and megalithic chambered tombs were important to the cultures of the New Stone Age, not for interment of the dead, which they say was incidental, but perhaps for magico-religious reasons. The extravagant dimensions of long barrows, and the practice of only burying a relatively small (1-25) number of people, always beneath the broader end of the mound, help to support these theories that it is the structure rather than the remains contained within that matter.

Although Neolithic man created precious few monuments to his culture, those found dotted about our landscape pose more questions than can be answered. Besides the tumuli, too numerous to mention but for the larger ones given names, there are two other earthwork structures even more enigmatic – the henge and the cursus, for want of better descriptions. Although the amateur archaeologist among the readers will glean little inspiration from a visit to even the largest of tumuli, he will probably struggle to understand what aspirations motivated the creators of structures with such staggering proportions as the cursus.

The linear features of the latter, which in some parts of the country are known to extend for several miles, consist of a ditch and banking arrangement, while the penannular henge is basically a central, relatively level area surrounded by a ditch and outer bank. One or more 'causeways' usually link banking with the central mound. It has been postulated (Childe), that the usual juxtaposition of both cursus and henge with long barrows suggests a sepulchral connection, and that if long barrows were reserved for important tribesmen, is it unreasonable to assume that henges were the funereal monuments to the common man? Perhaps as has been intimated, after cremation the ordinary folk were buried in a ring of pits sanctified by the outer banking. In fact some funerary artifacts have been unearthed at a few henges elsewhere in the country.

The amateur archaeologist fortunate enough to be living in Yorkshire is well-placed for studying both cursus and especially the henge. Around Ripon is to be found the greatest concentration of henges in Britain, where there are six within a five-mile radius of the city. Some are almost completely ploughed out, though still indicated on Ordnance Survey maps. One which is still virtually undamaged, is located (SE353735) half a mile south-east of the A61 on Hutton Moor, an area rich in burial mounds. This henge is a tenth of a mile in diameter, measured from crest to crest of the outer banking, which is up to ten feet in height. Another similar henge is to be found (SE361718) one and half miles south of the first. This was originally of comparable size but is now almost lost to arable farming activities.

Plate 3: The central of three Neolithic henges at Thornborough, north-east of West Tanfield. *(Cambridge University Collection: copyright reserved)*

The area between West Tanfield, on the River Ure, and Thornborough is also of great interest. About half a mile west of Tanfield, where the dismantled railway crosses the lane to Thornborough, earthworks will be seen extending a few hundred yards either side of the road. This is a part of a mile-long cursus, best seen from the air, which runs in a south-west to north-easterly bearing. The features of the ditch and banking are a little confused at this point, for a line of three henges (SE285795, SE288788, SE270800) half a mile apart, cut across the cursus at right angles. Again, the proximity of barrows suggests some crypto-ceremonial purpose for the earthwork.

Another possible function of the cursus may have been defence, in a similar manner that this form of structure was constructed by the Brigantes during the Roman invasion of the Pennine regions in the 1st century. The monks of the 11th and 12th centuries also used ditch and banking arrangements to delineate the boundaries of their religious estates. One such boundary ditch runs from near Capon Hall (SD868668) north-west for a quarter mile alongside the road from Malham Tarn to Langcliffe in The Dales.

The sixth henge in the Ripon group is at North Stainley, beside (SE291756) the A6108, where it is marked on the maps as Castle Dikes. This site has degenerated to the same extent as yet another feature which may be the remains of a henge, near Great Givendale, one and a half miles south-east of Ripon. This structure is marked on the map as a moat (SE337693).

As we have already learnt, the area of the North York Moors is fairly devoid of Neolithic settlements or earthworks, possibly for the reasons pointed out. Similarly in the south of the county, though important sites of Neolithic encampments are known, we do not find the earthworks in the manner of the henge or its linear cousin. This does not rule out the possibility that they once existed in the area, but industrialisation has eclipsed most traces that have been left in the landscape.

In the Yorkshire Dales however, we find a few well-preserved henges. Because of their isolation from major centres, these have escaped the fate of those further east and perhaps to the south. North-east of Grassington, the Yarnbury Henge (SE014654) is located at an altitude of 1100 feet only 250 yards from the road. It may be reached by taking a footpath through a gap stile in the wall, a half mile south of Yarnbury House, and then striking off due east across the pasture. The earthwork is to be found adjacent to the far wall and is some 100 feet across from bank to bank, while the southern edge displays what appears to be the denuded remnants of a causeway. On the side nearest the wall it appears that an excavation had taken out a section through the ditch and bank.

On Aysgarth Moor in Wensleydale is Castle Dykes (SD983873), yet another example of a henge, slightly ovoid and some 210 feet by 186 feet from bank to bank, and showing what seem like causeways on three sides. The banking itself is twenty feet across and nine feet high. This structure can be reached from the Aysgarth to Thornton Rust road by taking off up the stony track by Riggs House (SD996882) and tracing this west for one mile. The henge is positioned south of this lane on rising ground before this descends into Haw Beck. A similar, but much larger, earthwork is the Maiden Castle (SE022981), though this may have been defensive. It is located in Swaledale just 300 yards south of the Grinton to Askrigg road over Harkerside Moor. It has two barrows associated with it as well as another nearby earthwork, and is 300 yards across.

Although the cremated remains of man have been unearthed from several henges around the country, unquestionably demonstrating some form of sepulchral function for these sites, it is no proof that this was the original purpose of these or indeed any other similar structure. It has been shown[3], by excavation and dating, that compound henges such as Stonehenge evolved over a thousand years or more; they were added to and further modified by successive generations of settlers.

Some henges may have served as sacred enclosures or, as seems to be the case at Maiden Castle in Swaledale, performed the function of a fort. Contained within the central area are what look like the outlines of a few hutments, and the very substantial outer banking and ditch support the theory that this may have been a fortified site.

Around Maiden Castle are other earthworks as well as a number

---

[3]
Stonehenge Decoded (Gerald S Hawkins)

of tumuli, tending to suggest a prehistoric importance at Harker Hill (SE024975). Most of the structures here, half a mile to the south of Maiden Castle, on the south-east flank of Harker Hill, take the form of earthen ramparts. One runs for almost a mile from SE020962 in a north-westerly direction to SE028976. Another linear feature can be seen (SE036982) where it can be traced for a quarter mile north from Dike House, crossing the Grinton to Askrigg back road. In the following chapter we shall look at the possibility that these structures on Harker Hill were adapted by the Celts merely making use of an existing facility.

*   *   *

Around 1800 BC the Neolithic race was infiltrated by bands of warrior farmers who arrived here from the Rhineland, bringing with them the next greatest developments in the civilization of early man since he discovered how to make fire. They brought with them a much finer pottery, the custom of single burial in round barrows and the technical expertise with which to produce tools and weapons fashioned from a gold-coloured metallic alloy. Initially combining copper with lead, and at a later date replacing the lead with tin, these Bronze Age invaders not only made arrow, spear and axe heads from the new metal, but it was also used for personal adornment. To some degree old flint tools remained in use for a considerable time. One can imagine only the more influential employing bronze tools and weapons, while the majority, including the Neolithic farmers, continuing to use flint.

Although the earthworks referred to as the henge is contemporary with the latter end of the New Stone Age, there is every reason to believe that they remained in use well into the Bronze Age, perhaps being modified with the addition of a ring of upright stones. Castle Dykes (SD983873) on Aysgarth Moor may be an example. Here, on a banking three yards high by seven across, a couple of large embedded stones are all that remain of what might have been a stone circle.

More important than the henge type earthworks, and certainly more evocative to the layman than anything else Neolithic man left to our imagination, are the great standing stones, the megaliths and stone rings. I have referred to them as rings since hardly any of them are ever truly circular in form, most being either flattened circles or egg-shaped.

The people of the Bronze Age are sometimes called the megalith builders. They migrated to mainland Britain from the Iberian Peninsula region of Portugal and Spain. It would seem, from the distribution of stone rings and standing stones, that this culture made landfall on the northern-most parts of Scotland and the west coast of England, and from these points gradually spread eastwards (see Fig. 1).

It is tempting to explain the almost total absence of standing stones in some areas by virtue of the local geology. Obviously it would have been fraught with difficulties to erect colossal megaliths in regions lacking massively bedded surface outcrops. Having said this we shall see examples where the importance attached to a particular site was such that it warranted transporting suitable material from sources many miles remote from the final resting place.

Some experts believe that the main factor that distinguishes the Bronze Age and earlier cultures was simply the use of metal. Others argue that it was the changeover to singular burials in round barrows. Today however, archaeologists seem agreed that it is not so much the style of barrow that sets the two cultures apart, but the treatment of the dead at the time of interment. The Neolithic man's belief in the spiritual aspect of the after life is elaborated upon in the Bronze Age. Those who excavate barrows have been able to identify several individual groups of Bronze Age settlers from their grave goods. These include weapons, personal decoration, beakers, food vessels and, at a later date, funerary urns were also used.

The Bronze Age people were farmers just like their predecessors but were much more efficient due to the introduction of the wooden plough. And if the distribution of round barrows is any indication, what amounts to a population explosion occurred. This took place over a period lasting about 1800 years. It has been estimated (Elgee) that in the North York Moors region alone there are about 10,000 round barrows. No doubt many more have been lost to time.

As is usually the case with burial mounds, the contents again prove of greater interest than the structure itself. Throughout the county there is a handful of important Bronze Age burial sites, which when excavated proved unusual to say the least. It became the norm during this period of the country's prehistory to provide the deceased with his every need for use in the life thereafter. Food and drink was often placed in vessels next to the body, usually placed in the foetal position with legs drawn up beneath the chin. One group of the Bronze Age culture became known as Beaker Folk because of their custom of including a solitary beaker in each round barrow.

At Seaty Hill (SD907656) two miles north of the village of Malham in the Yorkshire Dales National Park, is a burial site quite unlike any other ever found in Britain. The hill itself is not very lofty, some 200 feet higher than the surrounding countryside. But take time to stroll to its flattened summit and take in the magnificent vista. Looking east across Malham Moor towards Wharfedale, the ancient monastic highway of Mastiles Lane can be seen wending its devious route through broken limestone terrain. In the north lies Great Close Mire and behind this the large scar feature sharing the name. A little to the west, the reed-fringed Malham Tarn glints in the sun.

Standing upon Seaty Hill it is easy to understand why higher ground was frequently chosen for tumuli. Casting a glance about the hill top, all that can be seen today are the remains of a ditch and bank. This encircled a central area originally containing two conical pits about five feet deep, and linked by way of a narrow slit. When opened many years ago archaeologists discovered a skeleton seated in one pit peering, apparently, through the space into the neighbouring pit. The latter contained a beautifully built cairn of rocks. The whole had been covered over with a small mound over which a second, broader but quite low mound had been constructed. No grave goods were found, and Seaty Hill remains to this day a complete mystery.

Four other Bronze Age barrows are extremely interesting because of the manner in which the deceased were interred. In each case they had been laid to rest in what was either a canoe or dug-out tree trunk. At Howe Hill (NZ696188) near Brotton, the remains were found inside a decaying wooden coffin beneath a mound containing a boulder with cup and ring markings upon it. More of these enigmatic rock carvings later.

In 1834, a further round barrow was opened on the cliffs above Gristhorpe (NZ894189) some five miles down the coast from Scarborough. Inside, the archaeologists discovered a log seven feet long and three feet wide beneath branches from the oak tree. This was the lid of a hollowed log coffin in which the perfectly-preserved skeleton of a man had been laid out in animal skins, fastened with a bone pin. Grave goods included a bronze ring, a dish fashioned from bark and a dagger. These are on display in the museum at Scarborough.

The remaining two 'boat' burials are at Loose Howe (NZ703008) and five miles north of Skipton, at Scale House (SD971569) near the village of Rylstone. When excavated, the former site, located at an altitude of 1420 feet, revealed an eight-feet long boat-like coffin. The remains it once contained had long since disappeared, but left behind was evidence that the body had been dressed in linen and wore some form of leather foot covering. At Scale House the person had been interred wearing a cloak of woollen or similar finely-woven material.

Other notable Bronze Age barrows are to be found in Sleddale at Cod Hill Beck (NZ611124), at Scarth Nick (NZ469000) and at Obtrush Roque (SE662945), and further west at the mound of Stony Raise (SD951869), located on the southern flank of the 1564 feet Addleborough Hill in Wensleydale. The ones at Cod Hill and Scarth Nick both incorporated a kerb in the form of a ring of stones in the manner which was commonplace during the Bronze Age. However in the case of the Scarth Nick site, the total absence of suitable sized slabs or boulders was overcome by building the kerb of dry-stone walling.

Many of these early structures were the focus of local mythology, connected with goblins and giants. The famous tumulus of Obtrush Roque was according to tradition haunted by a goblin known as Hob, who seemingly was a familiar and troublesome visitor to local farmsteads. The naming of this barrow is probably derived from a lingering superstition brought to Yorkshire by the Norsemen, the Hobthrust or Hob O'the Hurst, a spirit who frequented woodlands.

At Stony Raise it was giants that the local people had to contend with. Here legend tells of a giant carrying a heavy chest full of gold across the fellside. At the site of the barrow he cried out. 'Spite of either God or man, to Pendragon Castle thou shalt gang.' The chest promptly fell from his grasp, sank into the peat and became covered in stone. The legend goes on to say that the chest can only be recovered by someone to whom a fairy appears in the shape of a hen; however, it must at all costs be spirited away in complete silence.

Throughout Yorkshire, countless less important barrows have yielded beakers, food vessels and urns. One of the latter was found in the Sheffield suburb of Crookes, and points to there having been a Bronze Age burial site here, though all trace has been lost. Settlements of Bronze Age are also widespread but two of the finest sites are to be seen at Iron Howe (SE527950), generally regarded as one of the best examples of Bronze Age enclosure walling in the North York Moors region. The second location is at Dew Bottoms (SD912692) by an old monastic track across Malham Moor. Hut and enclosure foundations can be clearly seen (see Fig. 2) though much more evident from the air. Yet a third important Bronze Age settlement exists at Green Crag Slack (SE130460) and on nearby Woofa Bank (SE143457) on the edge of Ilkley Moor.

Fascinating as the contents and circumstances of many Bronze Age burials may be, to the interested layman or amateur archaeologist

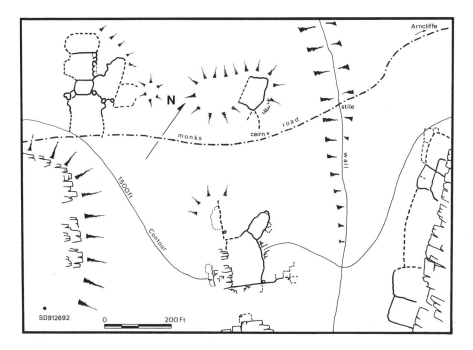

Fig. 2: Map showing the layout of the Bronze Age settlement site at Dewbottoms, in the Yorkshire Dales. Hut circles and enclosure boundaries are clearly visible on the ground.

who has never had the opportunity of participating in the opening of a barrow, the latter present themselves as featureless, denuded mounds, in many cases barely recognizable for what they are. Having said this, some hill top barrows, Seaty Hill being a good example, are worth a visit simply for the fine view to be enjoyed. The fact that some barrows are located on high ground commanding open panoramas, leads to the belief that at these sites we see the cemetery of important tribesmen, possibly chieftains.

                              *   *   *

Having looked at the tumuli of this period and compared their contents and layout with their counterparts belonging the Neolithic, we can move on to those most evocative of prehistoric monuments, the stone rings and megaliths. If the cursus and henges proved mysterious, the great megaliths standing in grim isolation, weather-scarred and defiant, are intolerably so. These timeless tokens to our ancestors have inspired more speculation than any other artifact.

The motorist passing Boroughbridge on the southbound carriage-way of the Great North Road, the A1, probably never spares a thought for the three blackened pillars of stone presiding over the fields just a few yards off the road. Chances are that few people even notice them, even though the highest of the group is some twenty-one feet high. These are the famous, nay legendary Devil's Arrows. The best way to see these megaliths is from the Roecliffe road out of Borough-bridge. The arrows are located (SE392665) adjacent to the road, one just through a gate on the south side and the remaining two in the field at the opposite side of the road just before reaching the A1 overpass.

Seeing the Devil's Arrows for the first time is a sobering experience. Standing beside these silent monuments to the aspirations of prehis-toric masons, one cannot fail to sense the immense age of the striated stones. We may wonder too, at the intense labour which, undeterred, overcame gravity to erect the stones for whatever the purpose.

The three stones are aligned along a bearing of 340 degrees, the northern-most being 300 feet from the centre stone, and this one some 200 feet from its neighbour across the road. Land use beyond the continuation of this bearing has eclipsed any signs that may once

Plate 4: The Devil's Arrows megaliths stand in farmland near Boroughbridge.

have existed to suggest that other stones formed part of the group. Both Leland and Camden knew of a fourth stone and there may have been more. It has been suggested (Bogg) that there could have been as many as twenty, though there is no evidence to support this.

Impressive as the Devil's Arrows may be, they are overshadowed by another standing stone at Rudston (TA097677), five and a half miles west of Bridlington. Located in the churchyard this impressive megalith is six feet wide and almost three feet thick and towers twenty-five feet above the tombstones. As such it is the tallest standing stone in the British Isles, and is only exceeded by a similar stone, known as the Great Menhir in France. Had this not toppled and broken into four sections, it would have stood sixty feet high.

Although the arrows at Boroughbridge and their larger cousin are the only standing stones in Yorkshire that live up to the image of a megalith, there are also many smaller stones thought to date from the same period. The largest of these in the North York Moors is called the Hanging Stone (SE585929), located on Roppa Moor, a six-foot stone alas no longer upright. A glance at Ordnance Survey maps covering both the North York Moors and The Dales areas will reveal the names of many other isolated stones or small groups, some of which almost certainly date from the Bronze Age.

On Malham moor a half mile to the east of Bordley, three standing stones are marked on maps as the Druid's Altar (SD949653). Seen from a distance they appear not unlike a group of grazing sheep, yet close up their true nature is revealed. Apparently this is all that remains of a much depleted stone ring standing on a banking fifty feet across. It bears some resemblance to a 'four-poster' – a monument more usually associated with Scotland.

Other similar collections of stones, some being incomplete rings, are the Cammon Stone (SE625000), located on an ancient moorland track from Kirkby Moorside to Ingleby Greenhow, the Long Stone (NZ983968), Wade's Stone (NZ830131), the Druid's Circle (SE983968) and Old Wife's Neck (NZ905022). The latter is a standing stone some six feet high, forming part of an open arrangement of stones associated with earthworks on Fylingdales Moor.

Bride Stones, too, is a name which frequently crops up, sometimes applied to natural outcrops of rock, while others are most probably of Bronze Age origin. Examples in the east of our area are High Bride Stones (SE850046), which is the last vestige of at least one stone ring, Low Bride Stones (NZ845048), which may be the remains of an old walled enclosure and Bride Stones (SE575980), part of a degenerated megalithic tomb. There is also a Bride Stones Moor (SD932268) north of Todmorden near the Lancashire border though this is quite definitely natural.

In the Wolds the principal Bronze Age settlement seems to have been at Garton Wold (SE985615) near Driffield, with smaller, established encampments at Boltby (SE506857) in the Hambleton Hills. Others are suspected to have existed in the Pickering and Whitby areas. In the Yorkshire Dales National Park the largest stone ring is located in Wensleydale at Oxclose Pasture (SD990903) near Carperby. This is an almost complete ring measuring 94 feet by 78 feet, but unfortunately all the stones are now recumbent. In the same valley a smaller 'circle' can be seen near Redmire village three miles east of Carperby.

Other rings can be examined at Farncarl Hill (SE064631), a fine example beside the River Wharfe at Yockenthwaite (SD900794) and three are to be found on Ilkley Moor. The best preserved of the Ilkley group is the Twelve Apostles (SE126451). As the name would imply, this is formed of a dozen gritstone slabs and boulders, mostly three feet high, arranged in a vaguely ovoid form. Two of the stones at the east side are now fallen. The nearly perfectly circular Yockenthwaite ring is very likely based on the surviving kerbstones of a Bronze Age round barrow, the mound itself long since weathered away.

To reach the Twelve Apostles, follow the obvious footpath leading past White Wells (SE118467) from Ilkley, which takes a route slightly west of Ilkley Crags and passing Gill Head (SE124459). At this point a boundary stone can be seen on the skyline ahead. The stone ring is located 400 feet south-east of this beside the track to Horncliffe Well and Baildon. The ring at Yockenthwaite (see Fig. 3) is much more easily reached by crossing the arched bridge and following the Dales Way path northwards along the east bank of the river for half a mile.

Having given the reader the opportunity to visit and contemplate these great monuments, how can the laying out of these strange groups of stones, or the erection of huge monoliths such as that at

Rudston, be reconciled with a culture regarded as primitive? What purpose drove these people to such feats of engineering? As we have seen earlier, henges were sometimes associated with burials, whether or not these earthworks were originally intended for this purpose. In the immediate vicinity of rings and standing stones no evidence has ever been discovered that might reflect a possible function, or shed any light on methods of construction.

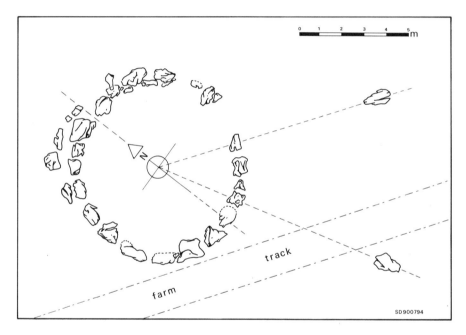

Fig. 3: Layout of the Bronze Age stone ring at Yockenthwaite in the Yorkshire Dales.

Some rings we have seen were the kerbstones for barrows, referred to as cairn circles, and were possibly set out as such to mark out and contain the material from which the burial mound was constructed. It is also possible that the ring was adopted for ceremonial purposes for some time prior to the building of the mound. Other free standing stone rings though, are monuments in their own right and pose archaeologists with one of their greatest unsolved puzzles.

Many theories have been put forward to explain the function of rings; everything from corrals for containing beasts to prehistoric calculators for predicting the movements of the heavenly bodies. Many amateur investigators of prehistoric remains go to great pains to prove that stone rings are linked to astronomical alignments. There are so many stars in the firmament that there are bound to be some that line up with the stones! The truth of the matter is, however, that no one really knows for certain why they were erected. The almost clinical barrenness of most sites is thought by some to be the principal clue to the whole mystery. Perhaps the central mound was sacrosanct, where fertility ceremonies or other important functions were presided over by a sachem. The ditch could have served to prevent the uninitiated or ordinary people from entering the central arena when they came to witness events.

At the Rollright Stones, a ring of seventy-seven stones in Oxfordshire, a team of investigators in 1979 participated in an experiment called the Dragon Project. Intriguing claims had been made that circles and megaliths were focal points for the earth's energy. The group reported to have detected ultrasonic waves emanating from within the weather-beaten stones at around dawn.

Stones as energy transmitters, sacred dancing arenas or sacrificial temples, all manner of explanations have been suggested for the existence of the thousand or so rings and megaliths scattered around Britain. Despite this, archaeologists and scientists are no nearer a solution to the riddle locked within the stones. Could it be that rings and megaliths are little more that primitive representations of the male and female reproductive organs? Megaliths are certainly phallic.

If we cannot agree on a possible function for these stones, we can at least guess at the methods adopted to erect them. It is clear that primitive cultures were quite able to erect huge stones weighing several tonnes. Thor Heyerdahl, during his expeditions to Easter Island showed that with a dozen men, some wooden poles and piles of rocks, it took only eighteen days to erect a fifty-tonne megalith. In 1938 too, an operation to re-erect the 'Barber Stone' at Avebury, was successfully accomplished under the direction of Alexander Keiller.

What of the giants at Boroughbridge and Rudston? In the case of the latter it can be assumed that to be stable, the stone would need to have at least one third of its length buried in the ground. Since the Rudstone megalith stands twenty-five feet out of the surface this would suggest a total length of over thirty-four feet. How could a culture only recently introduced to the use of metal have manipulated a stone such as this?

At first sight the problem would seem insuperable but in reality is simplicity itself. Firstly they would have had to dig a hole of a suitable depth, a task not requiring any ingenuity. One side of the pit would probably have been formed into a ramp, while they may have reinforced the opposite side with timber to prevent the stone digging into the side and jamming when it was slid into position. Once this was achieved the pillar was straightened and the hole backfilled and tamped down.

If this seems an incredibly simple operation, what is not so easily explained is why these Bronze Age farmers often chose to transport stones for several miles, as with the Boroughbridge and Rudston sites. What was so special about these places that the raw materials had to be dragged overland? Why not build their monuments where the materials were available? We shall never know the answer to this conundrum. We can however guess at where the stone was obtained.

A glance at the geological maps of the region reveals that for the Devil's Arrows the nearest sources of stone, millstone grit in this instance, were at Brimham Rocks (SE210649) or Knaresborough (SE350750), some eleven miles and six miles respectively as the crow flies. However the nearest gritstone outcrop to the Rudston is on the coast at Cayton Bay (TA070845), fifteen miles to the north.

Legend explains how the Devil's Arrows arrived at their present resting place at Boroughbridge. The inhabitants of nearby Aldborough, site of the Roman town of Isurium Bragantium, apparently incurred the wrath of his Satanic Majesty in the dim past. In his rage he proceeded to the summit of a nearby hill and set up a great bow. Chanting the words 'Boro-brig keep out o' the way, for Audboro' town I will ding down' he loosed his colossal arrows. Fortunately for the people of the town, they all fell short of their mark.

Julius Caesar attributed monuments like Stonehenge to the Celtic Druids, others ascribing the erection of such mighty works to the Romans themselves. They were renowned for engineering feats of this nature back in their homeland. Until well into the 17th century it was either the Celts or Romans who were given the credit for all these monuments. One legend places responsibility for those great stones on Salisbury Plain with King Arthur's Merlin, who it is reputed helped transport the materials from Ireland by setting up his 'engines', presumably some form of supernatural power.

Plate 5: Foundations of the south wall at the Roman Isur Bragantium (now Aldborough).

In the case of Yorkshire's own megaliths there was no such magic or machines involved in their movement, and certainly no intervention by extra-terrestrial stone masons. The shifting of these large gritstones involved nothing more fantastic than brute force, some elementary engineering principles, the use of sledges and a certain amount of orienteering ability to find the route of least resistance.

From Brimham the route chosen for the Devil's Arrows might have been overland via Picking Gill to the River Skell, a course involving

the minimum of uphill country (see Fig. 4). Transferring the stones
to rafts, it would have been a simple journey downstream past where
Ripon is today, to the confluence with the Ure. The latter flows
alongside Boroughbridge. Being practical though, the Bronze Age
architects would more than likely have chosen to bring the stone from
the site at Knaresborough. This was obviously shorter and certainly
the more plausible route. It is possible that suitable stones were found
lying around, dumped there conveniently by retreating glaciers.

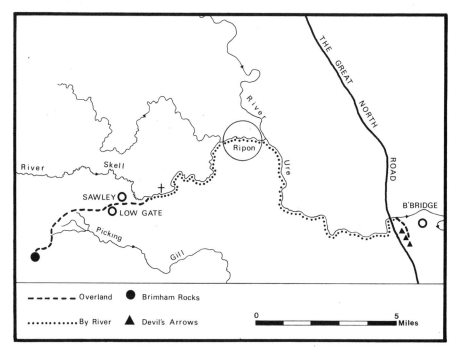

Fig. 4: Map showing postulated route of stone for the Devil's Arrows megaliths.

In delving for the reason behind the silent countenance of such
age-old stones, many people look for a deeper, more symbolic purpose. We believe, perhaps wrongly, that because the erection of these
monuments would have been so labour intensive, they must surely
embody some profound significance. But why has there to be a deeper
underlying purpose? The whole point about all of man's prodigious
works is that there does not have to be one.

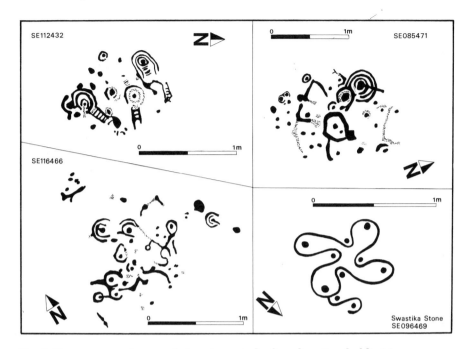

Fig. 5: Four groups of cup and ring stones to be found on Rombald's Moor.

We have seen how primitive man, once free of the mere business of staying alive, was at liberty to contemplate his environment, develop ideas and look at his surroundings more subjectively. Leisure manifests itself under many guises and early man, the megalith builder, created his stone monuments, not because it was vital to his well-being, nor for the fact that his tribe looked upon it for spiritual guidance, but simply that it pleased him. We could wonder today at the creations of 20th century Homo Sapiens, and what significance might be attached to them by archaeologists in, say a thousand years' time. What will our successors two millennia from now think of a pop concert video, egg painting or the enormously ornate temples built to the idolization of our Gods?

                    *   *   *

Finally, in this journey through prehistory, we shall look at yet another mystery left by the Bronze Age people for us to puzzle over. They are the so-called cup and ring stones, found in the greatest concentrations in Northumbria and on Rombald's Moor above Ilkley in Yorkshire. With one or two complex exceptions, these usually take the form of small hollows (cups), usually no more than an inch deep and from one to five inches across, together with either a series of concentric rings or groups of parallel lines resembling 'ladders' (see Fig. 5). They are often associated with barrows.

An Ilkley-based amateur archaeological group has, over several years, carried out a detailed study of the Rombalds Moor area, logging over 280 sites of cup and ring markings. These mostly consist of cups with rings, however a few sites display solitary cups.

Although examples are widely distributed across Rombald's Moor, Baildon Moor and Skipton Moor, the greatest concentrations are to be found at Rivock Edge (SE075445) and between Woofa Bank (SE142453) and Hebers Ghyll (SE094472) – Green Crag Slack in particular. Two compound examples are quite elaborate and have been given names: the Swastika Stone (SE096469) and the Tree of Life Stone (SE180504).

The last-mentioned site is to be found at Snowden Carr on the north side of Wharfedale, one and a half miles north of Askwith. It consists of a series of cups and interlinked scrolls, vaguely resembling a tree. It is suggested by some to represent the Norse *yggdrasill* (Tree of Life), though it predates the Viking Era. The Swastika Stone is also a composite arrangement, in this case eleven cups and curling arms bearing a similarity to a cross.

These rock carvings have baffled archaeologists for generations. The nearest examples remotely similar to the Swastika Stone are to be found in Sweden and Italy. The first recorded observation of carved stones on Rombalds Moor (Wardell) was in 1850; some twenty years later their archaeological importance was recognised. In early 1982 the world leading authority on prehistoric art visited Ilkley Moor and was excited by what he found.

Though he was unable to improve on the many theories already expounded to explain the origin and purpose behind the Swastika Stone, Professor Annati did have thoughts on cup and ring stones. Though many of these are located in a context which suggests some link with Bronze Age burials, current thinking suggests a late Neolithic, early Bronze Age date. Annati believed them to be primitive symbolic diagrams of the solar system, which implies some elementary knowledge of our planetary system thousands of years before the science of astronomy was invented.

For the reader who would like to examine at first hand the work of these Bronze Age masons, Rombald's Moor is the best place to begin. Some of the finest examples of cup and ring marked stones are the Badger Stone (SE110460), a large outcrop at Hangingstone Quarry (SE128468) and another stone south-east (SE075446) of Dobrudden caravan site.

Winter is the best time to search for the carvings, since many of the stones are low in the ground and, in summer, the mantle of heather, bracken and crowberry can make finding them almost impossible. I have spent fruitless hours on hot summer days, thrashing through thigh-high vegetation. But do not despair dear reader, if perchance you fail to locate any carved stones the first time. A few examples were relocated: one to Keighley marketplace; another is set into a dry-stone wall at the Dobrudden caravan site (SE137401); and there are also the famous Panorama Rocks, which were moved in 1890 to their present site, a small railed-off enclosure in Queen's Road, Ilkley.

*   *   *

And there we have to leave the enigmatic carvings of Ilkley's famous moor, the earthworks and monuments of the megalith builders. It is up to you to draw your own conclusions. Is there some unfathomable religious meaning to any of these works, or is it that we merely see nothing more significant than prehistoric doodling, the work of a prehistoric Kilroy?

Why should there be any deep cultural point to any of man's aspirations, then or now? Travelling along the A65 Keighley to Kendal road along the western edge of the Yorkshire Dales, on the edge of Newby Moss, you may see a prominent cairn (SD729721) standing on Grey Scars. This six-feet-high, neatly-built pile of limestone rocks, overlooks the Wenning towards the Bowland Fells. What compelled person or persons unknown to build this structure where they did, and for what purpose?

The location commands a magnificent view. Could there be an

ancient burial beneath the pile, or does it simply mark the route of some long-forgotten prehistoric trade route? It looks out west, towards the coastline from which the Bronze Age people are believed to have come. Did these people build the structure in memory of the land they left behind?

In fact, the cairn was built many years ago by myself and a group of friends, while exploring pot-holes on the nearby karst plateau. It took the four of us an hour or so to erect – but for what reason? Because we thought it was a good idea at the time. We left no markings in stone or bedrock that would indicate who built it, when or for what reason. It simply pleased us on that day a long time ago, and today it proves my point that all may not be what at first it seems. Ramblers seeing the cairn may contemplate the structure in silent wonder. Who built it? Why?

3

Brigantia – its rise and fall

It is the sacrificial altar, fed
With living men – how deep the groans!
– Bryant.

While the status quo endured in Bronze Age Britain, ancient civilizations elsewhere in Europe and the Mediterranean were coming of age, warring with one another, and decaying. The Mycenaean Empire of Greece collapsed about 1000 BC, and while Britain basked in its isolation, great centres like Carthage, Gades (Cadiz) and Massilia (Marseilles) crumbled beneath the military might of Rome.

For five centuries before the birth of Christ, the Cassiterides (Tin Islands) as Britain was then referred to, had been known only to the most adventurous voyagers who set sail out of the Mediterranean, or from the ports of Iberia and Gaul. As far as the ancient cultures of the Mediterranean were concerned, the world extended no further than the Pillars of Hercules (Straits of Gibraltar), beyond which the edge of the world, dragons and even worse fates awaited those foolhardy enough to pass beyond.

Of all the early seafaring peoples of the Mediterranean only the Phoenicians had the skill and audacity to sail their vessels out beyond the limits of the known world. In 450 BC news of the Cassiterides reached Herodotus, that father of Grecian history, and was probably gleaned from the experiences of the Phoenicians. The name Cassiterides was derived from the Greek for tin, *kassiteros*. It was first recorded by Homer and may have been a Celtic word borrowed by either Greek or Phoenician travellers.

From these early Greek scribes we learn that between 500-400 BC a new culture was emerging as one of the most powerful races in western Europe. They were a tall, proud people with war-like tendencies, skilled in the use of iron and rode horse-drawn chariots into battle. They ranged over much of continental Europe as far as the shores of the Black Sea. In the year 390 BC their warriors sacked Rome.

Almost a century later their eastward progressing armies had ousted the Etruscans from the valley of the Po, in northern Etruria (what is now Italy) and subjected Delphi to their wholesale pillage. These highly successful warriors were referred to by the Greeks as the *Keltoi*, from which the name Celt is derived. Their remains were first identified from what had obviously been an important Iron Age cemetery, dated c.700-500 BC discovered in 1848 near the Austrian market town of Hallstatt, and later from a second site (c.500-100 BC) close to the shores of Lake Neuchatel in Switzerland at a place called La Tène.

It seems highly probable that the Celts had been plying the capricious waters of the channel over to Britain sporadically since around 600 BC, perhaps as itinerant merchants trading salt for Cornish tin. This was sought for use in the making of bronze ornaments for personal decoration. The Celtic races in Europe were being galvanized into a homogeneous movement, enjoying common cultural and linguistic roots.

Soon after the first contacts with Bronze Age Britain, there followed a more permanent migration. What motivated this, we cannot be certain. Perhaps they were merely furthering their expansionist designs on western Europe, the need for land to settle, or possibly the move was fuelled by some driving force that urged them to follow into the west the sun they are believed to have revered.

Enter now Iron Age Britain and with it the realms of recorded history. The Celts, we know, had a religious cast in the Druids, who though literate prohibited committing their cult and history to the written word. As a result we have to rely on Greek and Roman sources. From the latter, for example, we are able to identify many different tribal groups, such as the Belgae, the Iceni, the Coritani and many more. We are even provided with the personal identity of important individuals. Thanks to historians and geographers like

Strabo and Ptolemy, and the Greek navigator Pytheas, historical facts gradually enable us to augment our sketchy archaeological evidence to provide an insight into life in Iron Age Britain.

One thing that emerges concerning the Celts is that they owed no allegiance to any overall sovereign or Government, but consisted in the main of a collection of loosely confederated states. Two of the most powerful of these were well-established in the Yorkshire region by the first century. If we were to draw an imaginary line from the Wash across the country to Chester, everything north of here as far as the Scottish border counties, and including all of Yorkshire, was known as Brigantia. West of the Pennines (Cheshire and south Lancashire) and between the Humber and the North York Moors became the territory of the Cangi and the Parisii respectively (see Fig. 6).

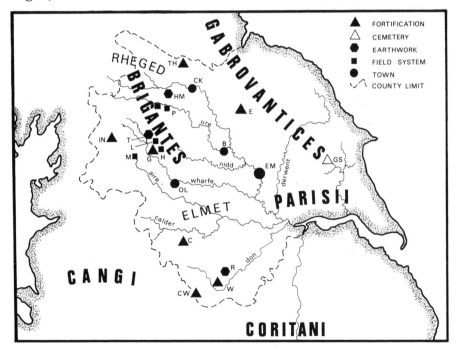

Fig. 6: Map of Iron Age Yorkshire indicating tribal territories and principal Celtic sites: TH) Toft Hill; CK) Catterick; HM) Harkerside Moor; P) Penhill; E) Eston Nab; IN) Ingleborough; T) Ta Dyke; L) Lea Green; M) Malham; G) Fort Gregory; H) High Close; B) Brigantium; OL) Olicana; C) Castle Hill; CW) Carlwark; W) Wincobank; R) Roman Ridge; EM) Eboracum; GS) Garton Slack.

The Parisii, or La Tène Celts, were essentially agriculturalists, and brought with them an iron-tipped ploughshare which was to give them an advantage over the heavier, clay-based soils of the lowlands. A climatic deterioration had by that time begun forcing the natives into the Wolds from the moorland regions to the north. Here, they would have been in direct conflict with the new settlers. The Brigantes on the other hand inhabited the higher, less-compromising lands of the central Pennines region.

Rising water tables in the Vale of York and similar low-lying regions, and the spread of bog woodlands that this encouraged, was to further exacerbate tribal pressures upon the habitable landscapes. Armed with the Hallstatt sword,[4] and with their experience in matters of warfare, the Parisii would have easily been able to overpower and subdue any opposition.

Throughout Brigantia the 'pecking order' would have been laid down by the more well-to-do Celts. Competition for all available land increased. The Celts with their improved tools would have cleared woodlands from the more desirable countryside, probably leaving the indigenous people to suffer subsistence on the old impoverished land.

Mixed farming was pursued within the constraints imposed by terrain. In the areas of better soil compositions, cereals for instance took precedence over livestock.

The fell country of the Pennines on the other hand presented a geography that was more suited to the pastoral lifestyle of the Brigantes, although the discovery of a few querns in some areas, Wharfedale in particular, suggests that they too cultivated some grain. The climate of the Pennines must have resulted in a landscape similar to that of today; one can imagine the difficulty of attempting an arable economy in a landscape more suited to raising livestock.

Remains found at the site of settlements suggest that the domesticated breeds were represented by goats, pigs, cattle, horses and sheep. Evidence supports the continued farming of these upland areas even during the wetter Iron Age. Like the Bronze Age people, the Brigantes

---

4
  First identified in 1848 from the town of Hallstatt in Austria

were quick to recognize the benefits of settling on the better drained limestone terraces and pastures of the northern Pennines.

Despite the obvious superiority of the invaders, it seems improbable that a sudden revolution took place, and with it the wholesale slaughter of the megalith builders of the preceding Bronze Age. For a while both cultures probably co-existed, and gradually over a period of time there would have emerged a new Iron-Bronze ethnic caste. Except for a minimal amount of woodland preserved to meet the everyday needs of weapons, house building, fuel and tools, it was no longer practical to retain the extensive tracts of broad-leaved timber, notably alder and birches. And so the de-forestation begun by the Bronze Age farmers was continued with even greater resolve through the Iron Age.

Given that the arrival of the Celts had been a peaceful affair, the British Isles must by virtue of its geography, have remained comfortably insulated for countless centuries from the true horrors of organized warfare. By the year 55 BC however, the curtain was being raised on a period of British history that was to have profound consequences for the future of its inhabitants.

*   *   *

Sometime during the late 4th century BC Pytheas, the Greek explorer from Massilia, sailed north along the western coast of Europe and made a daring voyage around the coastline of Britain. Rome no doubt heard via travellers such as Pytheas of this wild country beyond the seas to the north-west of Gaul. As early as 57 BC Julius Caesar had designs on a military campaign against Britain, inspired by a belief in vast mineral wealth or bounteous grain fields.

In late August of 55 BC a sea-borne force of 10,000 troops sailing under his command was directed toward the southern coast of Britain. They were returning from a military campaign against the Germanic tribes of north-western Europe. Caesar was well known for his caution in military matters, that it seems amazing he should choose this moment in which to pursue, without prior preparation, his latent desire to conquer Britain. In the event his army made landfall on the southern coast of England, their beach head being in the territory of the Cantii (from which the name Kent is derived) near

Deal. It was an operation doomed from the outset, given the lack of planning and his ignorance of British inshore waters.

Having chosen low tide in which to despatch his forces ashore, Caesar's men were forced to wade the last 100 yards or so under enemy fire from bows and slingshots. As might be expected, this first encounter with the Britons was little short of a disaster; the transport ships bearing his cavalry were delayed and when they finally arrived most ended up scattered by a sudden storm, other ships either floundering or dragging their anchors to be wrecked against each other or nearby rocks.

By this time, Caesar had probably recognised his error. He was unable to advance inland. Faced with many months in hostile country until sufficient ships could be salvaged and made seaworthy, his main concern was for the well-being of his troops. Replenishment of essential supplies was not made any easier by the bellicose nature of the Cantii warriors. While repairs were affected Caesar ordered their encampment to be fortified and *catapulta* and *ballastae* to be brought from the dismantled ships.

Patrols and foraging parties sent inland each time met with misfortune, the Celts falling upon them unexpected after laying in hiding in the woods. The Romans suffered heavy losses and quickly discovered to their detriment how effective was the use of the Celtic war chariot. Thus the invaders were repelled without so much as glimpsing an ear of corn.

Caesar followed up this abortive landing with another invasion force in the winter of 55-54. Again they suffered similar set-backs with the capricious channel weather, food again was scarce, the morale of the legionaries was low, and yet again he was faced with a humiliating withdrawal. The autumn of AD 54 was the season of discontent in Gaul, exacerbated by failed harvests and increasing demands upon available resources made by the Roman forces stationed there.

The growing insurrection among the Gauls was to occupy Caesar's thoughts for the next fourteen years, and as it happens these events saved the Cantii from further attempts to annex their land until, that is, the invasion of AD 43 sanctioned by Claudius. Upwards of 40,000 conscripted soldiers were disembarked on the southern shores of Britain, heralding a long period of colonial rule for the native Briton.

By the time the first Romans arrived in Britain the Celts and their culture were well-established throughout the country. Ptolemy records that towards the close of the first century AD these people had established several important 'towns'. In Yorkshire, these were to become the sites of Romano-British settlements or forts, sometimes given Romanised names such as Isurium Brigantium, which is today's Aldborough. The other British towns were Olicana (Ilkley), Eboracum (York), Cataractonium (Catterick) and Danum (Doncaster). Only the last two retain names that resemble their original form.

What do we know about the extent of Celtic influence in Yorkshire, and what more might be gleaned? The Romans found, as we have already said, that a mixed farming economy was pursued throughout the territory of both the Brigantes and the Parisii. For their own ends the Romans would have sought to encourage the continuity of this practice, even if under the Roman yoke. In a few localities the outline of field systems reflecting the pattern of farming in the Iron Age can still be seen by those prepared to leave the car behind and proceed on foot. There is no finer way of exercising than by combining rambling with the added interest of history and archaeology.

In the Yorkshire Dales National Park area the best preserved and most easily reached Iron Age sites are those to be found at High Close (SE005655) and on nearby Lea Green (SD996663), both near Grassington in upper Wharfedale, and at Malhamdale (SD896638) overlooked by the 300 feet high Malham Cove. At each of the above locations, excellent examples of field systems date from either Celtic or the later Romano-British period. They have survived the subsequent veneers of the Dark Ages, the Norman Conquest and almost a thousand years of modern hill farming activities. That any visible remains have survived at all is little short of a miracle.

Those in the valley bottom pastures at Malham can be seen to advantage in the famous view from the top of The Cove, easily attained by a well-made footpath up the left (west) flank. The best time to see these is winter, when a low sun angle produces extended shadows, 'etching' into relief the pattern of tiny interlocking enclosures cradled in the fold of the valley below. Please don't be carried away by the view to the extent of neglecting caution near the edge, it is a one-way trip down!

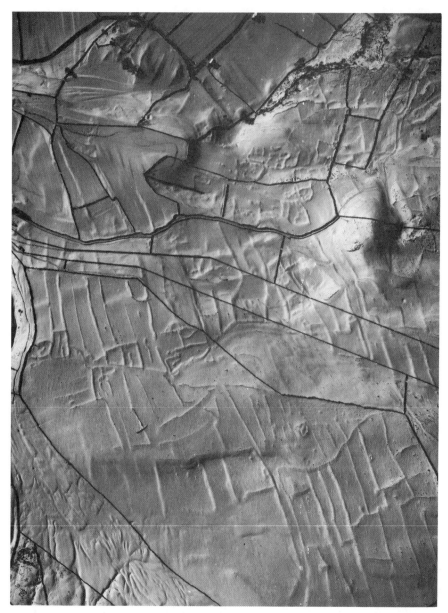

Plate 6: Aerial view of High Close near Grassington, Upper Wharfedale. The low sun angle clearly highlights the Romano-Celtic field system of enclosures in the lower and central parts of the picture. *(Cambridge University Collection: copyright reserved)*

At High Close, an area approaching 300 acres is clearly distinguishable on the ground extending northwards from Grassington up a shallow valley towards Sweet Side. These appear as ranks of rectilinear earthen mounds corresponding to the old enclosure boundaries. Moreover, the area is crisscrossed by numerous tracks, no doubt very old, some of which must surely be contemporary with this period.

To reach High Close, leave the town's Main Street by the Town Hall, turning left along Chapel Street. Just over 400 yards along here a path branches to the right (signposted Dales Way) by a farm. A field path can be traced from here for half a mile. After crossing the first stile the first signs of Celtic enclosures appear. They become more obvious, and after the third stile the regimented mounds of field boundaries can be seen marching forward and over the wall to the right and beyond Bank Lane.

The Dales Way long distance route bears left from the third stile, but another footpath continues straight forward, uphill with a wall over to the right. The Lea Green remains can be reached by following this path for nearly a mile. When a pond is reached just before the route leaps a stile on the right, strike west to find Lea Green remains a few yards away. The mounds and tumbled remnants of a perimeter wall (see Fig. 7) enclosing hut foundations and pounds is really one of the truly evocative sites in The Dales. According to local tradition the last to inhabit Lea Green was a witch called Dolly Gill, who is supposed to have occupied a hovel some three hundred years ago.

When standing in the midst of remains such as those at Lea Green it is tempting to speculate on what form their dwellings adopted. Fortunately we are not confined to guesswork. According to Strabo, the Celts occupied dwellings that were round in plan with a central hearth and which usually had storage pits dug into the floor. The walls apparently were fashioned from roughly adzed planks, set end-on and placed side-by-side, to support a thatched roof. It was a pattern very nearly continuous with those used in the earlier Bronze Age, and indeed is similar to ones still used today by ethnic groups in some Third World countries, Papua New Guinea being one example that springs immediately to mind.

In the North York Moors the foundations of typically Celtic huts are to be found at several localities. Some of them are contained

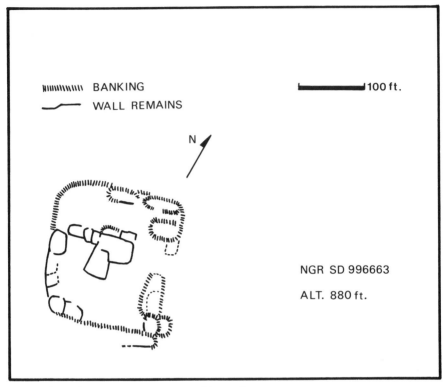

Fig. 7: Plan of Lea Green Romano-Celtic settlement.

within an outer enclosure that served a defensive function. Examples can be seen on Borrowby Moor (NZ766144), at Sleddale near the banks of Codhill Slack (NZ609119) and on Levisham Moor between Little Griff (SE833924) and Dundale Pond (SE829919). At the Sleddale site the circular outlines of five houses, each almost thirty feet in diameter and with flagged floors, are positioned near the centre of a three-hundred-feet-long enclosure.

Following a winter visit to one of the moorland sites of Iron Age occupation, I could not help dwelling upon the appalling conditions that must have prevailed during the darker months of the year. The inside of the huts must have been unbearably smoky due to the open, flue-less fireplace, yet this would have been infinitely preferable to freezing to death when snows were drifting around the walls. It makes one thankful for heat at the touch of a button, as a retreat to the car is called, leaving the sad remains of the hut circles to their ghosts.

Two additional locations in the North York Moors region are easily accessible for examination. The first of these can be clearly seen (NZ621109) adjacent to the road along the crest of Percy Cross Rigg, one and half miles north-east of Kildale. The site enjoys wonderful open views south and south-east over to Baysdale and Commondale, and north-west to the shapely cone of Roseberry Topping. Curiously enough, the settlement is situated on a high point of the ridge called Brown Hill, but more about the significance of this shortly.

Two miles away on Great Ayton Moor is an enclosure, square in plan, also dating from the Iron Age and which may have offered protection to dwellings, though there are no obvious signs of any. This is located only a half mile north-west of Oak Tree Farm. Another much more interesting place, this time at the opposite side of the Vale of York, can be seen in upper Wharfedale.

This site shows up prominently on aerial photographs and is also clearly visible on the ground. It is slightly south of the village of Kilnsey at Outgang Hill (SD971669). An oblong enclosure (Fig. 8), some one hundred and fifty feet by a hundred, contains the foundations of five hut circles of the style described by Strabo, each around twenty-five feet in diameter. Two smaller enclosures exist in the northern corner. Next to this is a slightly larger compound, around two hundred square yards in extent, while over the nearby wall in the pasture to the north-east, a field system covers approximately 1000 square yards.

Other groups of hut circles and field systems attributed to this period, can be studied in the parallel valleys of Wensleydale and Swaledale. Here the Iron Age is well-represented on Addleborough Hill (SD950875), again near Stony Raise (SD952869), and above West Burton (SE031860) to the south of Dove Scar. Two additional sites that invite a visit, are found at Arngill Scar (NY914014), where hut foundations occupy a ledge overlooking the River Swale, flowing here through the impressive Kisdon Gorge.

Seven miles down the dale, there is another site on Harkerside Moor close to the Maiden Castle (SE022981). Here we find a few hut circles contained within an outer perimeter banking. The site is generally believed to date from the late Bronze Age, though it is possible that the site saw co-habitation between Bronze Age native and Celt, or was an adaptation contemporary with the early Iron Age.

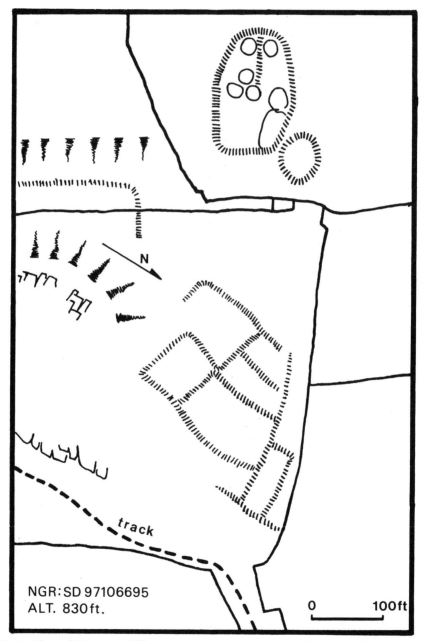

N

NGR: SD 97106695
ALT. 830 ft.

0   100 ft

Fig. 8: Plan of Outgang Hill, aerial interpretation of prehistoric settlement site possibly dating from the Iron Age.

Other earthworks dating from the later period exist in the vicinity, and this together with the fact that the name 'maiden' incorporates the Celtic place-name element 'dun' meaning a fortified place, seems to lend further weight to the assumption that the Celts made use of an existing facility. This is just one instance in which place-names can provide clues to the past.

The system of farming pursued by both Brigantes and Parisii was mixed arable with livestock rearing. Barley, oats, flax and rye were all cultivated, while the domesticated animals were represented by sheep, cattle, goats, pigs and horses. Grazing was confined to swampy areas of the lowlands and loftier regions of the North York Moors and Pennine regions, the better land being reserved exclusively for cereal crops. Wharfedale has produced several querns, proof that an arable economy existed concurrent with a pastoral lifestyle.

In the south of the county, evidence for Iron Age farming activities has until fairly recently been rather sketchy but, with the introduction of infra-red photography as an archaeological tool, many new sites of farmsteads, enclosures and settlements have been discovered. This method of investigation is beyond the scope of the amateur but the study of conventional aerial photography is accessible to the reader fortunate enough to have access to a collection of local authority aerial photographs or even a light aircraft.

When viewed from a sufficient altitude and under optimum conditions the outline of sites can be clearly revealed. A low sun angle helps to highlight the relief of the landscape, including prehistoric remains; at other times, a light dusting of powdery snow can show up the countryside below, just as French chalk makes a fingerprint visible. Following a period of prolonged draught, not so rare in this country these days, crop markings also help.

How the latter works depends on the state of the substrate. Where, for example, this has been disturbed in the past, as with ditches, pits or post-holes where buildings once stood, the soil is less compacted and holds moisture far better than the surrounding soil or that forming mounds or bankings. This is why during dry spells grain crops and grasses on the lines of ditches or holes continue to flourish while those around and about become stunted. This difference in growth rate shows quite clearly from the air, enabling the outlines of earth works, barrows, camps, settlements and such like to be mapped.

Plate 7: When seen from altitude crop markings can reveal the outline of settlements and other earthworks. *(Cambridge University Collection: copyright reserved)*

Not all sites discovered by these methods have been positively dated to the Iron Age, neither are the techniques restricted to detection of sites from that period; it works just as well for settlements as old as the neolithic. Either way though, these locations rarely present any visible features for the ground-based investigator. This technique has also revealed sites of suspected Iron Age around Malton, in the southern area of the North York Moors, though again these are not visible on the ground and fall outside the scope of this book.

In our quest for the roots of the county's past, there is an amazing oblivion to the fact that evidence is all around us, often on our very 'doorstep'. Within our hybrid language, for instance, there are components reflecting earlier cultures. That any Celtic place-names have emerged from the Teutonic invasions of the Dark Ages and even the blitz krieg colonialism of the Normans is a measure of the lasting

Plate 8: Crop markings at a site (NZ022656) near Kilham, North Yorkshire. The round feature near the top of the picture may be a round barrow. *(Cambridge University Collection: copyright reserved)*

influence Celtic culture had on settlers like the Anglo-Saxons and Danes. Several place-name components were handed down, though not always without change. An examination of these enduring signposts to the past can enliven a day out for ramblers in the Celtic territories of Brigantia.

An analysis of individual elements can provide the historian with an invaluable 'tool' to aid him in his search for Yorkshire's mist-shrouded beginnings. Sadly however, centuries of agricultural activity and urban construction have obliterated valuable evidence, bulldozed into oblivion in furtherance of 20th century 'progress'. Taking a close look at place-names is like travelling backwards in time, yet this needs to be tempered with caution since first impressions are not always reliable. However, if we are skilful in interpreting what we find, a great deal can still be gleaned about our ancestors, the lifestyle they led and about the landscape that supported their culture.

That Yorkshire has the lion's share of unusual names is apparent on examination of a map. What, for instance, might tourists make of Wombleton, Thwing, Crackpot, Giggleswick or the Land of Nod? Amusing though these and other names might be, in more practical terms the geographical distribution of more specific groups of place-names can suggest possible migration routes or provide clues to the pattern of early settlement. They have been bequeathed to us by way of a dim but invaluable reflection of cultures long since vanished.

Many hills and other locations include the name *pen*, the Brythonic dialect of Celtic meaning 'head', which means the head or summit of a high place. Examples in our region are Penyghent Hill (SD838735) in upper Ribblesdale, the town of Penistone (SE245032) in South Yorkshire, Pen Howe (NZ856037), on Sleights Moor south-east of Grosmont, Penrod Hill (NZ625129), near Stokesley and two instances of Pen Hill, one (SE471904) near Kepwick and again in Wensleydale (SE051867) near West Witton. Even the name Pennines is Celtic.

Other names believed to have Celtic origins include the common-place occurrence of Brown Hill. This includes the element *bryn* or *bron*, usually applied to a more gentle, rounded summit. The Celtic site previously referred to at Percy Cross Rigg (NZ621109) at Kildale is located on just such a hill.

The word *camb*, is another instance of how our present place-name terminology has harboured evidence lingering from Celtic times. It refers simply to a ridge. Camp Hill (SE058165) near Scammonden Dam, west of Huddersfield, and Great Coum (SD702836) overlooking Dentdale may be two distorted examples. Great Coum is the mid-point on a long ridge terminated at either end by Crag Hill and Gragareth. Contouring around the Dentdale flanks of Crag Hill and Great Coum is an ancient track, the Craven Way, linking Ingleton with Dent via Kingsdale. Was this 'road' part of a long distance trading route in use by Brigantian itinerants?

Guy Ragland Phillips[5] ponders on the probability of a pre-Roman

---

5
Brigantia, (Routledge & Kegan Paul)

route running the full length of the western side of the country from Cornwall to Galloway. We know that flint and stone tools continued in use for a long time after the coming of the Celts. It was probably only the more affluent of the Celts who used the superior iron weapons and implements, tin therefore remaining very much in demand by the peasants. Perhaps an ancient route did exist along which Iron Age entrepreneurs carried on a trade in tin from Cornwall and stone axe heads from the Lake District sites at Langdale. Is it so hard to imagine one such Celtic entrepreneur naming the hill that the trail circumnavigated? At the head-waters of the River Ribble there is a whole medley of further examples of camb including Cam End, Cam Fell, Cam West End and Cam Rakes. A scrutiny of large-scale Ordnance Survey maps will no doubt reveal others.

*   *   *

Throughout the region we are concerned with in this book, there are place-names identified with Celtic sources. Included among these are Rotherham, Fangfoss, Glaisdale, names beginning with Eccles (from the vulgar Latin for church, *eclesia*) and Otley's popular playground, The Chevin. This is almost certainly a time-warped version of another word meaning 'ridge' and is similar in pronunciation to the Welsh Celtic 'cefn'.

The once fashionable spa town of Ilkley is the Olicana that was eventually to hold such a strategic importance for the Romans, while the name Craven, for the upland region forming the southern part of the Yorkshire Dales, could be derived from the Celtic *craf*, referring to the wild garlic (Ramson) which still flourishes in wooded gills of the area. Further to the east, the North York Moors National Park has its Cod Hill and Cod Beck, both seemingly embodying the element *coed*, meaning wood in the Celtic tongue.

A much more interesting legacy of Celtic culture is the custom of burying the dead in barrows surrounded by a square ditch. This was a uniquely British phenomenon. One aspect of this that is highly significant and which inspired a great deal of excitement among scholars of Iron Age Britain, was the discovery of the so-called chariot burials. Wagon graves have their first appearance in Europe in the middle 7th century BC, where warrior chieftains were buried along with sides of beef and pork, horse bits and earthen vessels. It was a ritual imported from the Etruscans, and the oldest such burials connected with the Celts have been identified from Bohemia, Austria and Bavaria.

Some of the more detailed evidence of Iron Age influence in Yorkshire comes from the eastern parts of the region, along the southern fringes of the moors and again in The Wolds, where evidence of settlements from this period have been identified near Wetwang (SE934590). That the region abounds with square barrows suggests a strong spiritual element to their culture. These features are peculiar to the La Tène Celts and were apparently alien to the neighbouring Brigantes – further evidence of the strong division between the two groups. The Brigantes as we shall soon see, pursued their own overtly gruesome customs.

The excavations at Wetwang Slack (SE880580), some four miles west of Wetwang, and at another site at Garton Slack (SE953602), near Great Driffield, gave archaeologists a further insight into Iron Age cultures in the county and also provided many surprises. At these two locations, the Wetwang Slack one in particular, it was obvious from the extensive linear earthworks and barrow cemeteries, that here was a major settlement of the Parisii. As recently as 1984 three chariot burials, similar to those found elsewhere in Europe, were revealed by excavations in nearby gravel pits.

Archaeologists believed the earlier finds revealed nothing more fanciful than farm carts, yet the subsequent discovery of grave goods with obvious military connotations finally dispelled any doubts. In each of the Wolds burials, the chariot had been dismantled and the wheels and iron tyres placed beneath the carriage. Two of the barrows were quite clearly the graves of important warriors, for the deceased had been buried in a crouched position alongside their fine weapons and ornate shields.

Exciting as these discoveries obviously were, the third barrow was even more remarkable. This contained the body of a woman who had been laid to rest together with the riches of her station. She was well-provided for the after life. A side of pork had been placed beside her, together with a mirror, bronze box, horse bits also of bronze and several pins. It was obvious that here the barrow of some woman of noble lineage had been unearthed.

Many of Yorkshire's fine museums house artifacts reflecting life, and death in the Iron Age. The remains from these chariot graves can be seen on display at the Hull and East Riding Museum in Hull, where the Celtic World exhibit brings to life the La Tène culture of the Yorkshire Wolds. It is tempting to contemplate the ritual which must surely have accompanied the ceremonies accompanying these burials. Other exhibits include some fine Romano-British mosaics.

Julius Caesar's accounts[6] of the Celts describe one influential caste, the Druids (a name derived from the Greek meaning 'children of the oak') as men of elevated learning, absorbed with the contemplation of sacred groves, the moon, the sun and other heavenly bodies, but also bent upon appeasing their Gods in the most barbaric of manners. The Druid's pagan religion evolved a doctrine of immortality, a glorious life after death which no doubt goes some way towards explaining the daring courage of their warriors on the battlefield.

Their overt savagery even appalled the Romans, who were certainly no angels. The Celts were headhunters and, according to Diodorus, warriors hewed the heads of fallen enemies and hung them from their horses' manes, later to be preserved and displayed on the walls of their huts. More about this preoccupation with heads later. Some northern Celts, including those inhabiting Caledonia, tattooed their bodies or decked them out in blue pigment before engaging in battle. It was said to make them fearsome of appearance and thus they became known as the *Pictii* (the painted ones), from which the name *Pict* is derived.

Much of our knowledge of the Celts is owed to the Romans, but it is from them also that later cultures inherited a common misconception about this mysterious race. The Romans believed, quite incorrectly, that the so-called Druids were responsible for the erection of megalithic monuments like the stone avenues at Carnac in Brittany, Stonehenge, and probably our own Devil's Arrows, no doubt built to serve their pagan excesses in times of social stress. Standing stones

---

6
  De Bello Gallico. A translation of this is available in the Penguin Classics series under the title *The Conquest of Gaul*, revised edition, 1982

like those famous arrows were already ancient when the Celts arrived
and contrary to what the Romans believed could not, as we now
know, have been erected during the Iron Age.

This distorted picture of those learned High Priests of Celtic society
was embroidered upon by the writings of the Victorian romantics.
Cartographers jumped on the 'band wagon' so we find natural features
throughout the country that have been linked with what were imagined to be the pagan beliefs and practices of Iron Age Britain.

In Yorkshire there is a Druid's Altar (SE092400) on a prominent
gritstone outcrop overlooking Bingley in the Aire Valley, while near
the hamlet of Bordley, in the Yorkshire Dales National Park, a group
of three standing stones (SD949653) is variously marked on Ordnance Survey maps as Druid's Circle and Druid's Altar. This was
thought originally to be the remains of an embanked circle, or due to
its ruinous state, a small chambered grave. It has since been considered to be the surviving pillars of a megalithic four-poster, a burial
site of a type normally found in Scotland.

Others have conceived tenuous links between the Celts and the
more prominent and strangely weathered natural rocks. The celebrated gritstone outcrops at Brimham Rocks (SD210650) are no
exception. Just what the connection, if any, might have been between
these sites and the colourful image of the Druid is anyone's guess.

I would recommend a visit to the Bingley outcrop, or better still
the weirdly-eroded rocks at Brimham, but wait for one of those stormy
days for which the Pennines are well known. When the elements are
locked in battle and leaden clouds hang overhead like harbingers of
certain doom, it takes little stretch of a fertile imagination to visualise
these blackened, time-ravaged stones in use as sacrificial altars. Being
realistic though, it is unlikely that these exposed stations were the
scenes of bloodletting or other pagan customs. The stories are no
doubt good for tourism promotion.

Gruesome sacrifices were prevalent in Iron Age Britain, however.
We do know that some ritual interpretation manifested itself in
human votive offerings. These acts were more grievous than simple
blood-letting to appease immortal gods. According to Caesar we are
given to understand that the Celtic functionaries ordered huge hollow
figures to be built in human likeness, fashioned from the branches of

trees. Into these young men were herded and the effigy set alight in a ghastly carnage by fire. The auspices of the Celtic pantheon did not come cheap, for those unfortunates making the donations at least.

Curiously enough, in the tiny Wensleydale village of West Witton (SE062884) a quaint tradition bears an uncanny resemblance to the Celtic custom, though of course it does not include human immolation. The Burning Bartle ceremony takes place annually on the Saturday nearest Saint Bartholomew's Day (August 24th). A larger than life human effigy, fashioned of wickerwork and stuffed with straw (see Fig. 9), is paraded around the village streets until after dark, when it is burned on a bonfire to the accompaniment of a chanted rhyme:

> At Penhill crags he tore his rags,
> At Hunter's Thorn he blew his horn,
> At Capplebank Stee he brak his knee
> At Grassgill Beck he brak his neck
> At Waddem's end he couldn't fend
> At Grassgill End he made his end.

Exactly who or what was Bartle is, today, a mystery. He may have been the sheep-stealing giant who, according to local tradition, is said to have roamed on nearby Pen Hill. Perhaps Bartle was a spirit of the extensive forests that once thrived in the dale, or is he simply the faded memory of an ancient fertility symbol? Others (Bogg) have suggested that it represents the Saint, and though the timing of the custom appears to support this theory, one cannot entirely dismiss the vague similarity between this and the barbaric Celtic practice. Penhill is a further link in the cultural 'chain', incorporating the Celtic place-name component, *pen*, linking present times with the Iron Age.

In the year AD 43 the Roman campaign to occupy Britain began in earnest with the second invasion attempt. This began with the landing of four legions[7] under the command of Aulus Plautius. These were all battle-hardened frontier troops who, with an auxiliary force comprised mostly of cavalry, formed an invasion strength upwards of 40,000 men. It can be determined from these figures that the

---

7
A legion was a division of 3000-4000 soldiers

Romans were eager again to press on into the country north of the tribal lands of the Belgii and Cantii. Four years later Ostorious Scapula was installed as the new Governor of Britain.

Fig. 9: An impression of the Burning Bartle custom observed in the Yorkshire Dales village of West Witton. *Courtesy: Andrew Forrester*

The south of England was by this time almost subdued. But the Silures, in what today is Wales, stood their ground to the continued embarrassment of the invaders. A favourite Roman military tactic, that of dividing and demoralising the enemy, was put into effect. Accordingly, in the years AD 47-54, Ostorius started to drive a wedge of troops towards Chester, thus separating the Welsh Celts from those in the Midlands. Northwards from the latitude of the territories held by the Coritani and Iceni, however, the Roman advances were continually frustrated by the fierce tribes who inhabited the unknown lands beyond. This was Brigantia, where the natives sought guidance from a plenitude of pagan deities invested in the natural features of their rugged landscape.

The three basic elements of the earth and the firmament, those of air, fire and water, have been objects of veneration in all places from the earliest of ages. In these we have evidence in support of the earliest forms of ritual ceremony. The classical writers at the time of the Roman conquest recorded that groves, rivers, and especially wells and springs, were sacrosanct to the Celtic spiritual well-being. Ordeal by fire has already been highlighted as one method by which they solicited the will and cooperation of their gods. Others existed. In Yorkshire we have the clearest evidence that a water cult persisted throughout Brigantia.

Many rivers in Yorkshire have retained their original Celtic names – Ouse, Derwent, Esk and Aire, for example. Some were dedicated to the patron water nymphs, for instance Verbeia is believed to be the ancient name for the Wharfe, named after its goddess. Others reflect the clarity, mood or other aspect of the watercourse, as in the Nidd ('brilliant water') and Don (from *dana* meaning swift-flowing). Interestingly, the fort established by the Romans by the River Dana was given the Latin form of Danum, thus carrying forward the British river name component to be preserved in the modern Doncaster ('fort situated on the Don').

Altars consecrated to pagan divinities have been discovered in various localities. The Ilkley altar bears an inscription which reads "Sacred to Verbeia: Clodius Fronto, prefect of the Second Cohort of Lingonions (set this up)". A second dedicated altar was found at a river shrine near Bowes.

Not only were rivers the sacred abodes of beneficial spirits, but even springs and wells held a special place in the magico-religious order of the Druids. In Brigantia votive objects in various forms were cast into watery places. In the sleepy hamlet of Giggleswick, near Settle, there is evidence to support the theory that here an important centre of Brigantian worship once existed. The hamlet is situated at the centre of three ancient wells. Just a short stroll from the church of Saint Alkelda is the well at Bankwell (SD813639), covered with a stone slab and pouring its water into a stone trough.

Plate 9: The Bankwell Figurine was found at Bankwell, near Giggleswick. It is presumed a votive offering dating to Celtic times. *(Courtesy: Tom Lord collection)*

Towards the end of the last century, a small lead figurine was found in the well. It is about 7.5cm high and was once housed in the defunct Pigyard Museum, in Settle. It is now in private ownership. Due to its appearance the figurine was believed to be a toy dating from Tudor times. It was recognised, however, that some of the crudely executed features parallel a similar style of decoration found on a bronze shield contemporary with the La Tène culture found in a hoard at Merioneth. The similarities are so identical as to rule out coincidence. Moreover, it is even postulated that the Bankwell figurine may represent the Celtic goddess Brigantia herself – suggesting that Giggleswick church stands on or close to the site of an important pagan shrine, possibly dedicated to this deity.

The church at Giggleswick is generally associated with the nearby Ebbing and Flowing Well (SD803654), whose strange fluctuations have baffled travellers for centuries. It is not unreasonable to believe that this site, too, would have enjoyed some importance in those days and received its share of votive offerings. It still does if the number of coins and other objects found in it are any indication. At some time in the past all the wells in Giggleswick have enjoyed fame for their healing waters, including the Holy Well on the site of Giggleswick School next to the church.

Plate 10: The curious action of the Ebbing and Flowing Well has baffled travellers down the centuries.

Built into the fabric of St Alkeldas in Giggleswick can be seen two carved stone heads, obviously much more ancient than the building itself, and which may originally have come from a heathen shrine at either of its three wells. One head forms a corbel to an internal arch, while a second specimen has been incorporated into the outer surface of the north wall of the nave, where it gazes coldly in the direction of the Ebbing Well a mile away to the north-west.

These carved heads have been identified with a Celtic pagan cult[8] which persisted in Iron Age Brigantia, but we shall discuss this

---

8
Anne Ross *(Pagan Celtic Britain)*

further in the next chapter. Another matter, linked in some way with the Bankwell figurine, concerns the so-called naked man of Settle. At the western side of the market place is the Naked Man Cafe, formerly an inn of the same name.

It is an ideal place to take refreshments and a break from trudging about the local countryside in quest of our cultural genesis. Yet before setting foot over the threshold, look at the stone tablet on the wall above and to the right of the entrance. This is commonly referred to as the naked man. Exactly who this personage was and what the story is behind his apparent nakedness is not clear. However, there is something vaguely familiar about his countenance. The similarities between the Bankwell figurine and the naked man are more apparent that obvious, but it does provide thought for food while dining within!

Besides making votive offerings to lakes, pools and other aqueous features of the landscape, objects were also deposited in caves or cast down any convenient natural shaft. In Wookey Hole, Somerset, a famous instance was the discovery of several human skulls. Given the fact that Craven was at the heart of Brigantia one wonders what role, if any, the deep abyss of Gaping Gill played in Celtic paganism? It is easy to allow the imagination to drift back two millennia, to a scene of human sacrifice, victims cast into the depths of this frightful pot-hole as libation to the deities of the nether regions.

Within the cultural context of caves the significance of Attermire Cave (SD842642) leaves us in no doubt. Iron tyres of wheels, lynch pins and nails discovered at this site could simply have been the remains of a native wain, though its location in a cliff face remote from the nearest possible track makes this very unlikely. Somebody went to a lot of trouble to drag the vehicle up a steep scree slope, not easy to negotiate even without a burden, and to deposit it carefully within the cave. This is a sure indication of some ritual activity, despite the lack of sepulchral deposits.

Whether the Brigantes sought to affect the future in some sacred grove or watery shrine will never be known. Consultation with one of a multitude of gods undoubtedly strengthened their resolve in resisting aggressors from within their own culture, yet all the idolatry in the realm could not have prepared them for the ultimate doom brooding on their southern boundaries; the ascendancy of Brigantia was about to be challenged.

The Romans pressed on, heedless of the pagan beliefs of the natives. These were tolerated in the regions already pacified, but the Druids were loathed along with their role in a sacred order which completely mystified them. In the Druids, the Roman Governor may have recognised a means by which the barbarian tribes might be motivated in solidarity against their rule. They were certainly not afraid of death.

*   *   *

Possibly due to the bellicose nature of the northern tribes and the ruggedness of their domain, the occupying forces abandoned open conflict in favour of subterfuge in attempts to bring the mysterious Brigantes into the fold. The Romans made peaceful overtures to Cartimandua, their Queen, to whom they doubtless promised overall supremacy over her subjects once they had been brought under the influence of the Roman yoke.

It is thought that around this time the Parisii had also entered into some agreement with the Romans, allowing them to transport and sell their produce at military camps across the Humber in what is now Lincolnshire. It was a different story with the Brigantes however, the latter being bitterly divided on the issue of loyalty to the invaders. Cartimandua, (Sleek Horse) was pro-Roman yet her husband, Venutios, frequently castigated her for the growing allegiance to the enemy. She is believed to have had Castle Hill (SE152141), at Almondbury near Huddersfield, as her fortress headquarters. It commanded a fine position dominating the surrounding countryside for miles around.

These hill forts were highlighted by Strabo as one of the more obvious features of Celtic Britain. There are several fine examples scattered throughout the county, most of which are thought to date from between the sixth century BC and the first century AD. That some of these existed long before the arrival of the Romans is clear proof that domestic insecurities or widespread inter-tribal conflict was already prevalent. We cannot begin to understand the nature of these troubles for all documented evidence, from the hands of Roman scribes, naturally deals with the conflict as they had to face it.

In the North York Moors the fort at Eston Nab (NZ568183), appears to have started out as a Bronze Age fortlet which was later adapted by the Celts. Evidence suggests that the site had been long abandoned by the time the Romans arrived in the north. It is positioned on a scarp overlooking the Middlesborough suburbs of Eston and Normanby, one mile south-east of the A171.

Plate 11: Aerial view of a possible Iron Age fort at Eston Nab, North Yorkshire. The feature near the left edge of the rampart is a standing stone. *(Cambridge University Collection: copyright reserved)*

In the Hambleton Hills, two other forts occupied commanding positions. One existed at Roulston Scar (SE515815), above Sutton Bank, but this was levelled to make way for the runway of the Sutton Bank Gliding Club. A classic example of our nation's rich heritage having to make way for the whims of mankind. Slight traces can still be discerned at the edge of the cliff on the west side of the airfield and near the club house.

The second site, a little further to the north of Sutton Bank, is at

Boltby Scar (SE506856), one mile west of the well-known Hambleton Drove Road. The earthworks here were almost completely ploughed under in 1961, in yet a further act of contempt for national monuments. Today only a small remnant of the 'D' shaped rampart survives. This can be seen from the Cleveland Way long distance footpath which passes along the scarp edge. It is worth a visit if nothing else but to take in the wonderful vista. This extends west across the vast plains of the Vale of York to the high ground of the Yorkshire Dales, showing as a misty blue ribbon on the far horizon.

Among those distant hills, shimmering at the threshold of vision we find the most impressive of all Brigantian strongholds, and certainly the loftiest. Ingleborough Hill (SD743745) possesses an ambience that is most typically Pennine. Sweeping with sudden determination from its limestone plinth, a geological sequence of shales, Yoredale limestones and millstone grit rises abruptly to support a barren summit elevated at 2373 feet. Despite this modest height the view on clear days is sumptuous, extending across the Bowland Fells to Morecambe Bay, and beyond this to the Furness Fells and peaks of the distant Lake District in Cumbria.

Ingleborough, or simply the 'boro to local villagers, is thought to be the location of Rigodunum, a Romanised hybrid name of Celtic origins[9]. It may have been one of the seven Celtic 'towns' identified by Ptolemy. This aside, it is the most gaunt of the Three Peaks, famous with walkers and fell runners alike. Subject to capricious weather, its head frequently shrouded among swirling clouds and mists, it is a peak whose nature is reflected in the names of its rocky northern defences. Here we find The Arcs and Black Shiver, exposed scarps which at any time of the year offer the ultimate deterrent to a frontal attack, be it from walkers or Roman expeditioners.

At Bank Slack (SE219546), overlooking Fewston in the Washburn Valley to the west of Harrogate are the remains of defensive ramparts along a prominent spur close to Beaver Dyke Reservoirs. These earthworks may be the denuded remnants of a minor fort. Others are also believed to have been constructed during the Iron Age at Knares-

---

9
  Purported to be derived from the Celtic *Rig Dun* (King's Castle)

borough and Laverton near Ripon, though these have yet to be verified.

With most of the south effectively under the rule of Rome, the Welsh Celts, like many of their counterparts in Brigantia, had offered stiff resistance to the Romans. But alas, they too, were to fall victim to the ruthless onslaught of the well-armed and disciplined Roman legions. Caratacos and Togodumnos, once the proud chieftains of the Silures, were defeated like all before them.

Caratacos fled the mountain valleys of Cambria with the ringing of iron swords still echoing in his head, but it was with false hope that he repaired to the Pennines seeking the aid of Cartimandua. In her hour of treachery she sought to strengthen her perfidious alliance with the enemy by betraying Caratacos to the Romans. Venutios was furious and divorced himself of his wife. Caratacos and his family were eventually taken away bound in chains to be exiled in Rome, where he succeeded in winning their freedom, albeit confined to the city limits.

                                    *   *   *

In AD 61 increasing opposition to the Romans waxed among the hill tribes, while further south there was also rumour of dissent among the Iceni. Under the leadership of the Brigantian Queen's former consort all available military strength was marshalled in the valleys and hills for miles around **ingleborough**. This fact probably accounts for the abundance of small enclosures and hutments scattered throughout the limestone terraces of the Yorkshire Dales in that region. The winds of change were scudding across the northern hills like the wraith-like vanguard of impending disaster.

Those same zephyrs that sent cold, prying 'fingers' into every enclave of comfort at Rigodunum still send their chilly blast across the exposed summit of Ingleborough Hill. It is a worthy goal for anyone interested in the history of Iron Age Yorkshire and not simply for its Three Peaks charisma. There are four main routes to the top, though the shortest is from Chapel-le-dale with a starting point at the Hill Inn (SD743777). The walking is easy, but steep in a couple of places. Each year it is visited by thousands who trample the one square mile of its pear-shaped summit plateau oblivious to what lies beneath their Vibram soles. If only the time-ravaged stones could talk, how better informed we would be.

Those who gain the top with time to spare, and who have a mind for local history, will notice that there is something of greater interest than merely the expansive panorama from the triangulation pillar. Scattered about the relatively level summit, at the east and south-east sides, the foundation outlines of sixteen circular huts can be discerned among the hardy, windswept grasses (see Fig. 10). What we see today are the surviving ruins of what must have been a major bolt-hole for the hill tribes during the AD 61 revolt.

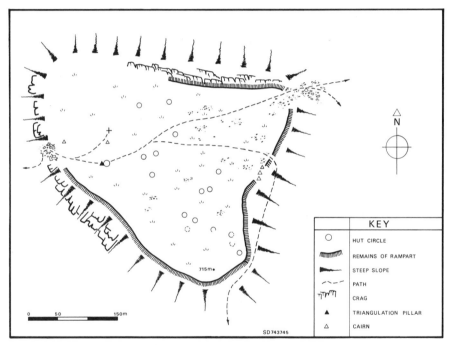

KEY

○	HUT CIRCLE
ᴍᴍᴍᴍ	REMAINS OF RAMPART
▶	STEEP SLOPE
‑‑‑	PATH
ᴨᴨᴨ	CRAG
▲	TRIANGULATION PILLAR
△	CAIRN

Fig. 10: Plan of the Iron Age hillfort at Inglebough Hill, possibly the site of Rigodumum mentioned by Ptolemy.

Circumnavigating this plateau, except on the north side where the plateau falls sheer at The Arcs, is an almost continuous line of gritstone rubble, all that survives of the defensive perimeter wall thrown up by the supporters of Venutios. It is gradually being spread about by the misplaced boots of the ignorant. It is easy to see why the location was chosen for its strategic and easily defended aspect, yet surely the harsh Pennine winters would have precluded occupation in all but the milder summer months.

In support of Cartimandua's struggle to crush the revolt in her own 'backyard', the Romans built more forts in Brigantia. One of these was founded to the east of Leeds, at Lagentium (Castleford) with another some twenty-five miles south east of Almondbury, at Templeborough in Sheffield. There are no remains to be seen of the former and the exact location of the fortification is not clear, though evidence has been unearthed at a pasture called Castle Garth south of the church. The latter is believed to approximate the position previously occupied by that of the Roman encampment, which must have been located to secure the river crossing close to the confluence of the Aire and 'Calder.

The Sheffield fort was built with similar military reasoning, occupying the south bank of the Don (SK414914), where this flows through the centre of the present-day city close to where the Roman road Ricknield Street forded the river on its northward route from Chester. This was two miles downstream from the fortress held by the Brigantes at Wincobank (SK378910), which the Romans probably also sought to neutralize. Again, nothing remains of the Roman fort, a steel plant now occupying the site. The Roman name for the fort at Templeborough is also unknown, but what is certain is that it covered an area of some 200 yards by 120 yards and was protected by a deep ditch and vallum. The fort was initially constructed from timber, but later consolidated by rebuilding in local sandstone.

If we are robbed of ground details featuring the Templeborough site the converse is fortunately true of Wincobank. Of all the Iron Age forts to be found in the region covered by this book, this was certainly one of the more impregnable. It covered about $6\frac{1}{2}$ acres and was constructed in a commanding position on a south-west, north-east aligned ridge overlooking the River Don. An inner oval enclosure was defended with the aid of a ditch, earthen banking and rampart. The latter was built of rubble reinforced with a timber structure and the whole faced with dry-stone walling. In its heyday, in the 1st century AD, eight hundred soldiers of the Fourth Cohort of Gauls were stationed here, including 240 cavalry.

Among English hill forts, Wincobank is unusual in that some of the stones forming the ramparts have been vitrified. For reasons that are uncertain, some of the supporting timbers were burnt. The intense heat generated resulted in some stones being turned to this very hard, glass-like form. This is no case of an accident or fire resulting from attack by an enemy, but appears to have been a deliberate attempt to consolidate the defences. Vitrified forts occur frequently in Scotland but are rare south of the border.

Plate 12: Occupying a 2.5 acre site, the Iron Age hill fort at Wincobank, Sheffield held a commanding position overlooking the river Don. *(Crown Copyright/MOD)*

Wincobank is an impressive feature. Today, however, it faces a more formidable threat, the steady encroachment of city suburbs upon its flanks. Standing on the summit and 'switching off' to the advancing city, it is easy to cast glances about the massive ramparts and ditches and imagine the fort in its operational state. The soldiers garrisoned here could hardly have imagined that a worse foe than the Romans would soon be knocking at the door. One can only hope that the result will not be the loss of yet another nationally important monument.

As the storm clouds of dissent gathered over Brigantia, a series of deepening crises put the whole Imperialistic war machine in jeopardy. Queen Boudicca (incorrectly Boadicea) led a very determined uprising within the powerful Iceni tribe. In the ensuing bloodbath at least 70,000 Romans and their sympathizers are said to have been massacred, a fact born out by the results of excavation. The revolt among the Brigantes was also gathering impetus, when the IX Legion was suddenly withdrawn to the south to deal with the Iceni. This gave Venutios renewed breathing space with which to prepare additional defences.

At several places in the Yorkshire Dales, massive linear earthworks scar pasture and fellside. Though some are thought to have contributed to the warfare strategy of Venutios, it is possible that others could have served a defensive role long before the arrival of the Romans. Perhaps they were simply enlarged and strengthened to help counter the expected attack? Though many of these earthen ramparts and ditches have been somewhat denuded with time, they are nonetheless impressive. One can only be filled with admiration for the people who doubtless toiled in all weathers to construct them. The finest examples are to be found in Swaledale, near Grinton at Swale Hall (SE041980), Dike House (SE036982) and on Harkerside Moor (SE023970).

In Wharfedale, Ta Dyke (SD985755) is the more impressive structure. It is bisected by the modern road across Scale Park above Kettlewell. This evocative site forms an obvious, deep linear ditch and bank cutting across the col linking the shoulder of Great Whernside with Tor Mere Top, and extends for half a mile either side of the road over Lime Kiln Pasture into Coverdale.

Some five miles down the valley from Kettlewell at Grass Wood, a delightful mix of broad leafed trees rising steeply from the eastern bank of the River hides an Iron Age enclosure (SD989653). Put together from heavy stones it marks the place where the Brigantes had a small fortlet on the brink of Gregory Scar. Presumably this was held to safeguard the passage into Wharfedale from the Aire Valley.

Fort Gregory most probably was built by the population of nearby Lea Green and High Close, for whom it must have served as a bolt-hole in times of stress.

Wincobank was obviously the focal point for the Celtic military machine in the southern marches of their territory, but other satellite fortresses are known to have existed. Defensive structures have been recognised at Carl Wark (SK259816) close to the Derbyshire border between Sheffield and Hathersage. Again taking advantage of the natural topography, stone walls were built to link rock outcrops, thus encircling and securing a promontory fortlet which commanded the outlook over Burbage Brook. Another possible site for study is Camp Hill (SE058165), five miles west of Huddersfield. The name incorporates the Celtic component camb.

Earthworks similar to the ones in The Dales that might also have served to defend Brigantian positions, can be seen at Canklow Hill (SK434910), at Langsett (SE207007) and on Bradfield Moors (SK240898), midway between Ughill and Sugworth Hall. The geologist Phillips in a reference[10] to the fort at Wincobank, describes an entrenchment that runs uninterrupted from here for four miles, though in what direction he does not say. Traces of this may be what we see today as the Roman Ridge where it passes just north (SK405966) of Wingfield, again at Nether Haugh (SK422968) where it is bisected by the B6089, and a half mile to the north (SK428895) of Upper Haugh.

Inevitably, the Iceni met with a similar fate to that which befell the tribes further south. After Boudicca had been overthrown, the Romans once more focussed their military might upon the Brigantes. They established a new centre of operations at Lindum (Lincoln). This move was made in readiness for the next stage of their campaign to bring the Pax Romana to the Britons holding the northern hill country.

Seven years later, the Emperor Nero committed suicide, plunging Rome into chaos. News of the instability this had created spread out into the colonies. The legionaries at Lindum were in a state of chaos

---

10
  The Rivers, Mountains and Sea Coast of Yorkshire, 1853

and, possibly via the Parisii, rumours of uncertainty among the Romans and their conscripts eventually filtered through to Venutios. He seized the opportunity for action, and with preparations still incomplete, in AD 71 he launched his attack on Almondbury, ousting Cartimandua, from Castle Hill.

Stability eventually returned once more to the rank and file legionaries. To consolidate the military victories gained in the Midlands, the Romans pressed forward into the territories north of the Mersey-Humber latitude. A road (later to become known as Ermine Street) had been built from Lindum to the Humber. Marching northwards along this, the IX Legion under Petillius Cerialis reached and crossed the river to Petuaria (Brough-on-Humber).

North-west of here a continuation of their road, Deira Street, had been constructed as far as a point reached by their supply boats thirty-three miles up the Ouse. Here the IX Legion was joined by the II Legion, who had trekked there via Danum (Doncaster) and another northerly trending road to Lagentium, then by Calcaria (Tadcaster) and the Rudgate, thus avoiding the treacherous Humber crossing.

On the bank of the Ouse, where York stands today, a new Legionary Headquarters was established at Eboracum. This rapidly became the Roman nerve centre for the subduing of the **brigantes**. From this military hub, new roads radiated like the spokes of a war chariot wheel (see Fig. 11). It was to prove the ideal springboard for the advance northwards, and later may have provided some logistical support to the frontier garrisons billeted along Hadrian's Wall, though this is more likely to have gone by sea.

It seems highly probable that the Parisii, like the Romans, took full advantage of the Ouse waterway link to the North Sea. However, if a fortified encampment or settlement was indeed held here before the arrival of the Romans, as seems likely, all trace has now been lost. The evolution of modern York is the result of veneer upon veneer of settlements and defences built by successive waves of invaders down through the centuries. Its long history is well-documented and falls outside the scope of this work. It is however worth briefly mentioning the surviving remains of what became one of the greatest provincial capitals of the eRoman Empire.

The first structure was merely a turf and timber palisade fortress established under the directives of Petillius Cerialis in the first century. Between the years AD 98-117 this was improved and added to. It was later rebuilt in stone with gates and corner towers. The structure was sited in the angle created by the confluence of the river Foss and the Ouse, and was divided by the latter.

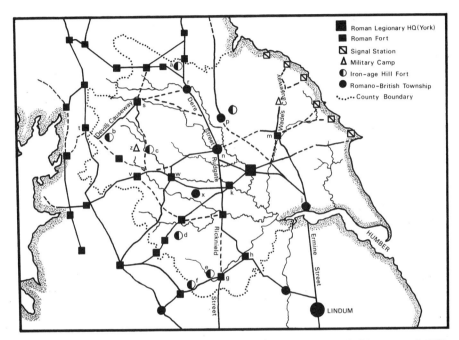

Fig. 11: Roman roads and other important sites in Iron Age Yorkshire: a) Toft Hill; b) Ingleborough; c) Fort Gregory; d) Castle Hill; e) Wincobank; f) Carl Wark; g) Templeborough; h) Danum; j) Barton-on-Humber; k) Tadcaster; m) Malton; n) Isur Bragantium p) Northallerton; r) Cataractonium; s) Virosidum; t) Overburrow; v) Elslack; w) Olicana; x) Adel (villa).

The main fortress, rectangular in plan, fronted the north-east bank of the Ouse with the *principia* (central headquarters) located where the magnificent minster now stands. In a space excavated beneath the central tower, visitors to the Minster can see remains of the Roman fort. On the opposite bank a *civitas* (civilian settlement) developed and included a legionary palace which was occupied by several Roman Emperors during their advance toward Scotland.

By the year AD 208 York had evolved into a thriving military and civilian centre. The Emperor Severus adopted York as his northern command post and later died and was buried there within the fortress walls. Later, the title of *coloniae* (colony) was bestowed upon York in recognition of its strategic importance in bringing the Pax Romana to the north. Today there are several places where the walls, several courses high, can be seen, with the best preserved being near the Anglian Tower and again at the Multangular Tower, next to St Leonard's Hospital.

From the writings of Tacitus we learn that, after her defeat, Cartimandua sought asylum in Roman-occupied Isurium Bragantium, where with her Roman hosts she plotted the downfall of her own people. With retribution against Venutios increasingly imminent he marshalled his allies into a state of readiness throughout the northern Pennines.

At Toft Hill (NZ181114) near Stanwick, some eight miles north of Richmond, a great fortress covering an incredible 750 acres, was put on alert. In terms of area it is easily the largest hill fort in Britain. The site can be visited from the nearby village of Fawcett, where the reader I am sure will find the shear scale of the ditches and stone faced ramparts one of the more impressive monuments to this period.

In the year AD 74, just three years after the storming of Castle Hill at Almondbury, Venutios came under attack along two fronts directed at Stanwick. The IX Legion under the command of Petillius Cerialis marched northwards out of Eboracum via Deira Street, through Isurium Bragantium and Cataractonium. Simultaneously the Tenth Legion completed the classic pincer movement by travelling up the western side of the Pennines. When the Brigantes were besieged by the Romans, their defence lines, despite their size, were little match for such ruthless adversaries. The Romans had the *ballastae*, war machines specifically designed for attacking fortifications. The result was a rout and signalled the end of the Brigantes' dominance of the Pennines.

The full horror of the onslaught was reflected in the excavations from Stanwick. Many human remains unearthed from the battlefield show positive and gruesome signs of the desperate hand-to-hand conflict that must have took place. What happened to Venutios is not certain, but those followers and vassals who were not slaughtered outright, or taken captive to work as slaves in the lead mines of Greenhow and the northern dales, sought refuge at hideouts scattered throughout the Pennines.

In the Yorkshire Dales the discovery of Romano-Celtic artifacts at Dowkabottom Cave (SD952689), Calf Hole Cave (SD964646) and Attermire Cave (SD842642) show the scale of their retreat. Sewell's Cave (SD785666), near Settle, revealed one complete and another incomplete Roman sword, also a fragment of possible mail plate which may represent battle trophies. Theirs was a lost cause, however, and as we shall see in the next chapter many Britons faced with defeat were eventually to welcome the Roman style of living.

4

A Tense Peacefulness

Dead are they, dead! – and I will go,
And for their sakes, come weal or woe,
Will lay the relic on the shrine.
– Wm. Wordsworth

Secreted within the remote northern hills, the Brigantes remained a
running sore as far as the Roman Emperor was concerned. They
continued to frustrate any possible northward advance, and it would
be some years yet before the barbarian tribes could be brought under
Roman influence. By AD 78 Julius Agricola had become the new
Governor of Rome's most distant and persistently volatile frontier.
Upon taking up office he immediately put into effect a plan that he
hoped would secure lasting control over the remaining pockets of
insurgents still at large in the Pennines.

Central to the success of this new offensive was the construction
of additional frontier defences and an integrated network of roads
with which to supply the legions garrisoned within them (see Fig.
11). More than sixty such fortresses have been recognised from this
period, and in Yorkshire include both those at Virosidum (High Seat)
in Bainbridge in Wensleydale and Derventio (Malton). All that remains at the latter site as reminder that a fort once existed are a few
meaningless grass slopes to the east of the town, a denuded reflection
of the defensive ramparts.

Unfortunately, very few sites of Roman forts in Yorkshire present
tangible remains to stimulate interest in the casual, ground-based
observer. In most cases all that can be seen are a few grassy undulations, unexciting except to the trained eye of the archaeologist. Some,
like the major fort at Templeborough, only survive in records, all trace

having completely vanished beneath urban development – in this case, below a steel plant.

Of all the forts built in Brigantia two of the more noteworthy are those at Ilkley (SE117479) in Wharfedale and the one at Bainbridge (SD937902). The latter straddles the top of the small but prominent Brough Hill that dominates the eastern aspect of the village, overlooking its large, well-kept green. On the summit some rectilinear depressions can be seen in which a few courses of masonry remain.

*   *   *

Down the centuries, Roman sites provided convenient sources of worked stone and they were frequently pillaged to provide building materials for later structures. The Saxon tower of the tiny church in Little Ouseburn, south-east of Ripon, contains quoins that came from ruined Roman buildings, as evidenced by the presence of Lewis holes[11] in some of the blocks. It is not known from where the technique originated, but it may have been used simultaneously by neighbouring Mycenaean cultures around 1500 BC. It is more probable that it was devised by the Etruscans, who were great engineers and used to handling colossal blocks of stone, and from whom the Romans gleaned much of their constructional know-how. It seems likely that the same fate befell Virosidum, stone being spirited away over the years for use in walls and early building work in and around the village.

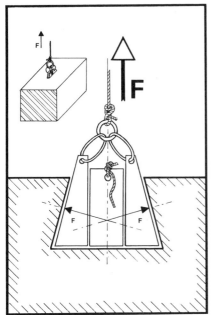

Fig. 12: Diagram indicating the Lewis hole principal of moving large blocks of stone.

11
   Lewis hole is a term used to describe a trapezium-shaped slot cut into large blocks of stone which, together with metal wedges, enabled the blocks to be easily lifted into place (see Fig. 12)

Looking at the military roads that lead to and from the fort at Bainbridge, the one from the Lune Valley is the most dramatic. Climbing out of Ingleton by way of Meal Bank, a spur sandwiched between the River Twiss and the Doe, the road quickly gains height. In somewhat less than a mile it turns north-east and henceforth heads up Chapel-le-Dale, deviating little from its straight alignment throughout the next nineteen miles.

Its course can be followed mainly along pleasant tracks, green lanes and quiet country lanes. From Meal Bank it can be seen continuing along the west side of the valley between Whernside and Ingleborough, perfectly straight as far as Chapel. Here the lane bends right to join the B6255 Ingleton to Hawes road, leaving the Roman alignment to cross the normally dry bed of Chapel Beck, before continuing as a hollow way to meet the main dale road near the old schoolhouse.

From this point, the Roman alignment is adopted by the B6255 as far as the former drovers' inn at Gearstones. Just beyond here a slight deviation takes it downhill to a ford over Gayle Beck (SD787803) from where it assumes its northeast trend. The road exhibits a slightly raised agger[12] as it climbs toward Cam End (SD802805), and here, at the centre of a magnificent panoramic view, a fingerpost indicates that the continuation is part of the 251-mile-long Pennine Way.

For my money the most inspiring section of the Roman way is from this point onwards, passing Kidhow Gate (SD830834) and Cam Houses where it contours around Dodd Fell. Unfortunately, from here until Fleet Moss it continues as a metalled road, but by way of compensation offers fine views across Oughtershaw, the remote valley head of upper Wharfedale.

The remarkable aspect of this route is the marked disregard the Roman surveyor had for the rugged nature of the terrain, succeeding in maintaining a wonderfully direct course. The road reached a maximum height of 1911 feet at North Gate shortly before crossing the Buckden to Hawes moor road at Fleet Moss. From there, it proceeded along the flank of Wether Fell (SD857867), with Semerwater shimmering in the distance like a fathomless sapphire set in green velvet, the prettiest lake in all of Yorkshire.

12
   The cambered central part of the road

From Wether Fell the military road, known here as Cam High Road, continues as a walled lane straight as an arrow for more than three miles towards the fort at Virosidum. This directness often betrays the existence of a Roman road and provides vital clues to the probable course of others. In this instance, it also gave rise to myths.

Locally, the military road is known as the Devil's Causeway, linking it with a local legend in which a giant and the Devil settled a dispute by hurling boulders at each other from either side of nearby Raydale, vis-a-vis the Carlow and Devil Stones. Virosidum may have been the focus for other military roads and, commanding such a fine prospect of Wensleydale, it is at once obvious why the Romans chose the site for a fortress.

A road probably crossed Askrigg Common into Swaledale, where the Romans mined for galena. From there, it may have continued north to the fort either at Catterick or Bowes. If this is the case its course has yet to be determined. Another route from Bainbridge down valley is suspected but all traces of this have disappeared.

From the layman's standpoint, the fort at Ilkley is of greater interest. Most Roman forts followed a common layout, in plan appearing oblong similar to that of a playing card (see Fig. 13). At Ilkley the perimeter of the fort, roughly following such a plan, is defined today by Bridge Street, New Brook Street, Castle Yard and Church Street. The earliest structure again was a timber one. However, there were as many as five phases of rebuilding in stone. When in use the fort at Olicana housed a garrison of 500 auxiliary troops, mostly conscripts who formed both infantry and cavalry units.

To the rear of the All Saints parish church, and reached by way of Castle Yard, is a superb example of 17th century yeoman farmer's house. This is now the Manor House Museum where a collection of artifacts reflects local life in the Iron Age. Exhibits include Roman altars, gravestone and examples of carved Celtic stone heads. To the rear of the building on its north side can be seen an eighteen-yard section of Roman masonry, originally forming part of the west wall of the fort and showing some five courses high and four feet thick. In the nearby church a small archaeological dig some time ago revealed a further section, as well as some smoke-blackened Roman altars.

As a measure of the scale of the Agricolan campaign to pacify the Brigantian tribes, some 1300 miles of military roads were built

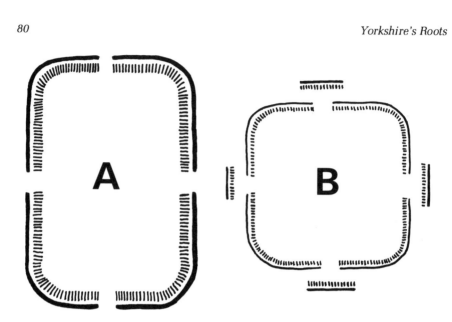

Fig. 13: Typical layout of Roman forts and military camps: A) The distinctive playing card shape of the fort; B) Plan of a marching camp showing the 'tituli' defending each entrance.

throughout the north, most surviving to form the basis of our modern integrated highway network. The accepted historical evidence, that the Romans constructed these roads, has recently been challenged by the radical view that a well-established road network was already in place when the Romans arrived; that Roman engineers simply improved and extended them. It is argued that since the Celts were clearly accustomed to wheeled transport, good roads would naturally have evolved.

The most important road in Yorkshire during the Iron Age became known in the Dark Ages as Deira Street, named after the Dere, an Anglian race who settled the countryside drained by tributaries of the Humber and which later became a province of Northumbria. The word is derived from the British *deifr* meaning waters. Deira Street appears on modern maps as Dere Street, and was effectively the northern continuation of Ermine Street beyond Eboracum, after it had made the difficult crossing of the Humber to Petuaria. Linking the legionary headquarters with Isurium Bragantium and Cataractonium, Deira Street eventually was to become the primary supply line to the northern-most outposts of the Roman Empire.

Plate 13: Looking north along Dere Street from near Aldborough. This military highway was of strategic importance to the Romans in their drive north from Eboracum (York). *(Cambridge University Collection: copyright reserved)*

It is clear from a glance at today's maps that the alignment of the Great North Road, better known to motorists as the A1, in part follows the course of Deira Street. Between Boroughbridge and Scotch Corner the line of the Roman road is taken up at the junction with the A61 (SE355762) from where it travels without deviation for some nine miles to The Poplars on the outskirts of Londonderry (SE306870). This is best seen from the flight deck of a light aircraft. From Londonderry, minor roads follow the line through Leeming Bar to where the Roman way is picked up again at Leases Grange (SE278915) and the A1 proceeds straight again until Catterick (SE241972).

Another military highway out of York is thought to have proceeded almost northwards, via Thirsk to Northallerton. Strategically speaking, however, next in importance after Deira Street were the ambitious trans-Pennine routes which, in the Agricolan period, were constructed to link Deira Street in the north and Ricknield Street in the south of the region, with another north-bound road running up the west side of the Pennines.

Leaving the A1 at Scotch Corner one of these roads crossed the Stainmore Forest, with forts at Lavatrae (Bowes) and Veterae (Brough), to reach Penrith where there was a third fortress at Brocavum (Eamont Bridge). This line is traced today by the A66 trunk road. Just a few miles north of here the Emperor Publius Aelius Hadrianus had his famous wall built.

Another route, later becoming known as York Gate ran from Eboracum (York) to Coccium (Ribchester), a distance of some seventy miles. At Calcaria (Tadcaster), a fortress safeguarded the ford over the river Wharfe, beyond which the road proceeded west. Its alignment can be traced in parts today, through the north Leeds suburbs of Alwoodley and Adel, then along the edge of Otley Chevin to the fort at Ilkley and beyond.

Just a half mile to the south of Eccup Reservoir York Gate passes through Alwoodley Gates. Alwoodley Lane runs almost straight and may be on the Roman alignment. The Roman road must have crossed King Lane near a farm of the same name, from where its most likely course proceeded to the Romano-British settlement at High Leas, Adel (SE278411). It seems to have been adopted by farm tracks and lanes from a point to the south of the Parkway Hotel (SE270413) to Wrinkle Hill Wood (SE252415) before crossing Cookridge Lane.

Passengers taking off from Leeds and Bradford airport at Yeadon, do so totally oblivious to the fact that Roman military traffic passed close by the north-west edge of the airfield almost 2000 years before flight was even thought of. Imagine too, what the Roman legionaries would have made of travelling inside the belly of great shiny birds and of the magicians who controlled them!

The continuation of the Roman road to the west is not clear, but is represented by Otley Old Road going by way of York Gate Plantation, following the edge of The Chevin across Guiseley Moor. Any possible continuation from there is hopelessly lost in the urban sprawl of Menston, Ben Rhydding and Ilkley, and not until west of Addingham does it become obvious again.

The road perhaps left Ilkley along The Grove and the present line of the railway as far as Addingham. From here it is adopted by a tarmac lane (SE065501) which gradually ascends to the edge of Draughton Moor. After a half mile the entrance to Upper White Well Farm is reached and the way ahead becomes a pleasant green lane contouring for three miles along the northern flank of Skipton Moor. For the walker it offers fine views across to Barden Moor and the conical summit of Sharp Haw. Soon the market town of Skipton comes into view and at a small wood (SE005510) dirt tracks coalesce before descending Short Bank into the town.

Continuing west, the Romans took advantage of the Aire gap, a natural break in the central range of hills, the route chosen probably coinciding with the track-bed of the disused Skipton to Colne railway, at least as far as Elslack (Olenacum), where a small fort was built c.80 AD. This covered an area of approximately 1.3 hectares and took up a commanding position as the base for an auxiliary cohort of 500 infantry men. Although the site is bisected by the railway, the Roman origins of Elslack (SD925495), otherwise known as Burwen Castle, were not confirmed until excavation was carried out in 1908 by Dr F Villy and a local vicar. Two phases were identified, the smaller Agricolan fort sitting inside a larger structure which was still in use in the 4th century. Discoveries including a coin minted in the time of Constantine I, potsherds and various items of jewellery which can be viewed in the Craven Museum in Skipton.

Little is known about the Elslack site, which occupies a slightly domed location protected on three sides by streams. The earlier fort lies within twin ditches and a clay rampart that was possibly riveted with turf. The later structure was the usual playing-card shape rather than the square plan of its predecessor. It was built to house the *Prima Herculea*, a cavalry regiment and covered 2.2 hectares.

It had a well-built, rubble-filled stone defensive wall almost ten feet wide at its base. Access to a rampart walk along the inside of this was by a clay ramp ten feet high and twice as wide. Excavation has revealed the existence of a substantial internal building which benefited from heating, the purpose of which has yet to be ascertained. A leaflet describing the fort is produced by the Roman Antiquities Section of the Yorkshire Archaeological Trust and is available from a nearby farm through which access to the Elslack site is permitted.

At least four other roads originating in Yorkshire travelled west across the Pennines. They were tenacious routes without exception. The one striking south-west from the fort at Virosidum has been briefly mentioned earlier. It probably provided a link to the fortress at Calacum (Overburrow) whereLeck Beck has its confluence with the Lune (SD615758), some two miles south of Kirkby Lonsdale. Another connected the Romanised settlement of Isurium Brigantium with Mancunium (Manchester). Yet another road out of Elslack is known to have climbed over the moors to the south-east, headed for some unknown destination in the Aire Valley where it joined the road to Manchester from Aldborough. Its course has yet to be proven but Street Head Farm (SD970473) may lie close to the line it took.

The course of the Aldborough to Manchester road across Blubberhouses Moor is marked on the Ordnance Survey map (Landranger Series Sheet 104: Leeds and Bradford). For some two and a half miles the A59 Harrogate to Skipton road travels in a perfectly straight line to a point one mile east of Blubberhouses. At a bend (SE184552) the modern road deviates around the north-western extremity of Fewston Reservoir, but the line of the Roman way continues beneath the reservoir before crossing the moors around Sun Bank.

When a change of direction was necessary, the Roman surveyor usually chose a place where elevation afforded a command of the surroundings. Thus, near Round Hill (SE128532) the road swings south, descending over West Moor. A glance at maps show that the road through Middleton has directional tendencies with the Roman alignment, however it is more likely that the Romans crossed the Wharfe at a ford which is believed to have existed close to the Old Bridge (SE112481). This uncertainty deepens as the road becomes lost beneath the streets of Ilkley, but the continuation south may be the stony track that is picked up at the top of town climbing steeply up Ilkley Moor, over Grainings Head to Cowper's Cross (SE102456).

*   *   *

The view northwards from this rough hewn monument is sufficient reward for the climb and extends to Almscliffe Crag and the radar dishes of Menwith Hill. At the very limit of vision beyond these, a hazy band of indigo can be seen hugging the far horizon on clear days. This is the tabular Hambleton Hills, the western-most outlier of the North York Moors National Park. When the sun is favourably placed the famous Kilburn White Horse can be seen glowing like a white hot beacon, its chalk strata reflecting the sunbeams.

From the radio masts at Whetstone Gate (SE102453), just beyond Cowper's Cross, the route turns west for half a mile, then south again to travel without deviation for over a mile. The line becomes uncertain from Riddlesden and not until Blackstone Edge is reached is it clearly visible, though it has been identified at isolated locations before that point. These are between Denholme and Denholme gate (SE069334 and SE069325) and north-west of Ogden (SE067310) where the line dives beneath Ogden Reservoir.

From this point, the alignment tends towards Midgley in Calderdale. However, the reader must journey to the Lancashire border on Rishworth Moor above Littleborough to see any positive evidence. The section of road crossing this wind riven landscape is without doubt the finest and most amazing of the whole road. Here, preserved almost as perfect as the day it was laid, is probably the best surviving example of Roman roadwork anywhere in Britain.

On Blackstone edge (SD972169) where the paved way cuts across a loop of the A58 Rochdale to Halifax road, the raised central strip of the road, the agger, presents features of engineering found on no other Roman road in the country. The section exposed is some sixteen feet wide and flanked either side by drainage ditches into which rainwater

run-off was enhanced by the provision of a cambered road surface. This consists of massive cobbles, hewn from local gritstone and bedded down between retaining kerbstones. They fit together with a precision that would astound any modern mason.

The unique feature of this road however, is found on its steepest gradient, a fact which may be the main clue to its purpose. Running down the crown of the road is a line of recessed slabs forming a channel some three feet broad. This addition, I believe, was

Plate 14: An especially well-preserved section of Roman road where it crosses Blackstone Edge on the borders between Yorkshire and Greater Manchester.

to provide a groove down which the brake pole of a cart could have been dragged. Signs of abrasion in the channel and the fact that it does not exist once the road levels out, is consistent with this theory.

The Romans were skilful engineers, having acquired and elaborated upon the technology used by the Etruscans, an ancient culture who settled in that part of northern Italy known today as Tuscany. It was from the masons of this dazzling civilisation that the Romans first learnt how to construct roads. The Etruscans built vast networks of roads and great processional highways linking city to cemetery and town to coastal ports. On some of these roads archaeologists have uncovered sections of causeway laid down with identical precision as that to be seen on Blackstone Edge.

If you imagine that travelling along some of these exposed routes was bad, spare a thought for the Roman surveyor and road builders who toiled in all that the Pennine weather could throw at them, to drive the road with little deviation up hill and down dale? The Pennine hills of Brigantia are a long, long way from Rome and the engineers must sometimes have felt that they would never see their home and family ever again. And many did not.

Yet a third trans-Pennine route ran from Tadcaster probably to Manchester via forts at Cambodunum (thought to be Cleckheaton), Slack and Castleshaw. The fourth road, believed also to have extended to Danum (Doncaster), went from the fort at Templeborough in Sheffield across the 'backbone' of England to Manchester by way of Stanage Edge. Here the route, now called the Long Causeway, crosses the border into the Woodlands Valley along which the Snake Pass (A57) today takes an almost identical course to Glossop.

The study of Roman roads and identification of, as yet, unknown sections is one branch of archaeology in which the reader could make worthwhile contributions. Many Roman roads today lie beneath our modern metalled highways, while many more miles are postulated but await confirmation. Valley floors in the Iron Age were often nothing better than swampy scrubland, the haunt of wild beasts. Because of this, the Roman surveyor would choose, wherever possible, a line that took roads along high ground, following ridges, spurs and sometimes the flanks of the dales. It was only when faced with no alternative that roads descended to the valley level.

Some stretches of these military highways survive as pleasant green tracks and bridleways, ideal for the rambler or amateur historian seeking clues to the past. It is easy when strolling along these ancient thoroughfares with only the elements for company, to project one's thoughts back and imagine the same scene nearly two millennia earlier. A case in point is the section of the York to Ribchester route between Addingham and Skipton. The Romans chose such a good line along the side of Skipton Moor, that in later years this was adopted as a pre-turnpike road into Skipton from Ilkley and Leeds. In 1769 it was travelled by the poet Thomas Gray on route for Craven.

*   *   *

At the turn of the first century, a brief peace embraced much of Brigantia except in the far north, where one must presume the Picts raiding out of Strathclyde prompted the building of Hadrian's Wall around AD 120 . The importance of many fortresses, for instance that at Catterick, faded once the wall was complete. That at Danum (Doncaster) was also vacated, but in the year AD 155 a major uprising among the Brigantes resulted in the wholesale destruction of some Roman defences, including the fort at Danum. Others which fell, but subsequently were rebuilt or repaired and re-occupied, include Bainbridge and Ilkley.

In the wake of this revolt, peace eventually returned to the region and was to endure for a further two centuries, a period referred to by historians as the Romano-British. The native who felt that way inclined soon became Romanised, many even adopting the Latin tongue. They were increasingly attracted by the agricultural lifestyle of the Roman economy. It was at this time that British settlements, the *vici*, evolved with forts or Romano-Celtic towns as their focus. This was very much the case at Catterick, Northallerton, Malton, Doncaster, Aldborough, Bainbridge and Ilkley.

Romano-British settlements have been recognised from several localities, in the southern parts of the county such sites being identified at Marr, Wadsworth, Grenoside and Hatfield. In most cases remains only become obvious from aerial surveys when the sites exhibit field systems similar to those seen to good advantage in the Yorkshire Dales at Malham and Grassington, and again on Addleborough Hill and Pen Hill in Wensleydale.

Attributed to this period are the so-called villas, including the site at Adel (SE278410). Far from meeting any preconceived 20th century notion of salubrious summer retreats for Roman officers, they were entirely owned and managed by Britons that had, for whatever reason, chosen the Roman lifestyle. These villas were principally agricultural establishments, administered more in keeping with the theme of the collective farm, but with a few concessions to Roman architectural innovation.

At least thirty such villa sites are recorded from Yorkshire. These are located predominantly on the rich alluvial soils of The Wolds region, and elsewhere, at Stancil (SK605960), five miles to the south of Doncaster, Gargrave (SD939536), Kilham, at Hovingham, Oulston and at Riccal Bridge (SE634841), between the village of Helmsley and Beadlam at the southern edge of the North York Moors National Park. Other villas are suspected but again in nearly every instance there are few, if any, tangible features.

Riccal Bridge is an exceptional site, easily accessible from the A170 just a mile east of Helmsley. Here the visitor with an interest in both Roman and Yorkshire history can see well-preserved walls, several courses high, tracing the foundations of buildings. Excavation by archaeologists showed the well-to-do Briton whose residence this was, enjoyed such luxuries as tessellated pavements, sanitation and a hypocaust or under floor heating system.

One of the finest Roman sites is at Aldborough. This was the Celtic Isur, one of the seven Brigantian towns referred to by Ptolemy and later renamed Isur Bragantium. Today the site is managed by English Heritage with two very fine tessellated pavements being preserved in their original location. Each reflects the luxuriously appointed interior to which its occupiers were accustomed. The third and probably finest of these mosaics is in Leeds City museum. It tells the legend of the founding of Rome and features Romulus and Remus being suckled by the She Wolf.

The perimeter defences of the Roman town completely encompass present-day Aldborough. Close to the site of its south gate can be seen the remains of an interval tower, as well as sections of the town wall, at this point almost 9ft wide. The foundation courses of the south-east corner tower are also preserved (see Fig. 14). Adjoining the site is a small but very interesting museum housing displays of remains unearthed nearby. There are examples of metalwork, coins, Samian ware, glass and carved stones.

Through aerial photography and the study of crop markings extensive areas in Yorkshire have been pin-pointed that were worked as arable farms in the 4th century and earlier. This fact coupled with the growth of settlements in which both Celt and Roman co-existed, and the discovery of numerous villas, suggests a period of prosperity that could only have flourished within a stable political climate.

The native Celt found this quiescence of the Pax Romana, and the more sedentary lifestyle that went with it, an ideal period in which to pursue and strengthen his relationship with the deities. There is little doubt that water cults endured in Brigantia before and probably throughout the Roman occupation. In its most overtly gruesome form, well worship focussed upon the severed human head. We know from reliable sources of the times that this was one of the symbolic

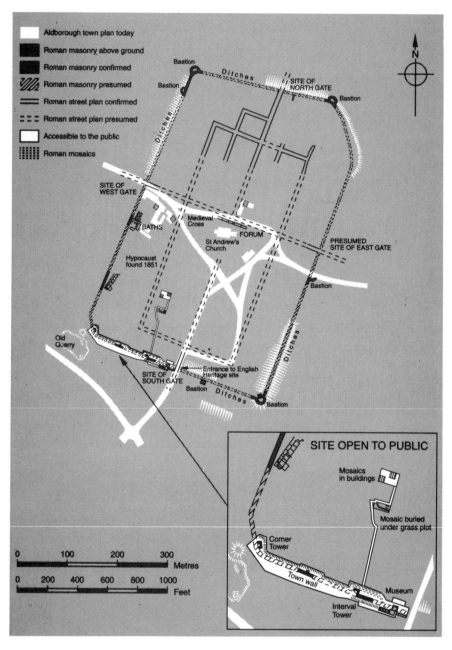

The Roman town of Aldborough (by courtesy of English Heritage)

mainstays of the Celtic culture, and as such was as vital to them as the crucifix today is to the Christian faith.

This preoccupation with head cults was not unique to the Celtic race. In cultures the world over the human skull has been regarded with superstition. Once severed, the head of an enemy ceased to be malign, and was considered to be of benefit to the well-being of its owner or the community as a whole. Former headhunters in Papua and New Guinea preserved the skulls and stuffed heads of enemies after relieving them from their owners as trophies or with which to consecrate a new *haus tamburan* (spirit house). Viking warriors too, drank from skulls in the hope of acquiring the valour of their foes.

Plate 15: The so-called 'Celtic Wall' located above Ribblesedale between Stackhouse and Feizor. Its purpose is unknown.

Perhaps as libation to Brigantia herself, the Druid order of Celts cast human heads into wells in the somewhat misguided conviction that this would safeguard the site, guarantee future water supplies and promote longevity! Though the Britons were quick to recognise the benefits of adopting the Roman way of life, they were not quite so eager to abandon long established pagan values. The result of this, amazingly enough, is that well worship has survived in various modified forms up to modern times. As we have already seen it is possible that Giggleswick stands on or close to such a heathen shrine.

The Romans obviously tolerated this state of affairs but with a more pressing need to assert Christian values. It is during the so-called Romano-British period that the first attempts were made to convert the natives to Christianity. The earliest form of the Ballad of Semerwater may have derived from these times as an early Christian morality story in attempts to bring into line the heathen community inhabiting the shores of the lake.

In AD 208 the Emperor Severus took up office in the imperial residence at Eboracum, a palace which is thought to have been located on the site now occupied by the railway station. York was by that time well-established as one of the strongest military and civilian centres in the Roman Empire. The Ouse waterway acted as the lifeline for this mercantile clearing house which enjoyed a flourishing international trade. It is believed that Alban became the first Christian martyr at this time, executed at the command of Severus' son Geta. Severus himself died and was cremated in York in the year 211 AD.

Nearly a century later, Christianity had begun to gain some ground among the northern pagans. In 311 AD, Flavius Valerius Constantinus was proclaimed Emperor at York. Though he was known to pay only lip service to Christian reform, he is credited later with ending the persecution of Christians throughout the greater Roman Empire.

Constantinus is best remembered as Constantine the Great, founder of the great Byzantine city of the same name. According to medieval tradition his mother was said to be the Brigantian princess Helena. Indeed it is attributed more to the influence of Helena that the Empire was Christianised at all. It is no surprise that many wells throughout the Yorkshire region were later sanctified in her name. A few of these retain their original dedication, as with St Helen's Well near Eshton (SD931571) and at Farnhill (SD005466). Another one exists on the south bank (SD032616) of the Wharfe some two hundred yards north of Burnsall. The Rag Well (SE453456) near Boston Spa was also known in earlier times as the well of St Helen.

Early missionaries were unable to convert many followers of pa-

Plate 16: A well at Farnhill, North Yorkshire, one of many such sites dedicated to St Helen.

ganism, so they absorbed the barbaric customs, renaming them to conform with the religious ideal, moulding them to fit ever so neatly into the Christian calendar. The sites of pagan wells were rapidly identified with Christian saints. St Chad's near North Ferriby for instance, is clearly a canonized pagan shrine for its waters have relinquished both Christian artifacts and objects dating from the Iron Age which were clearly gifts to some water nymph.

Votive offerings took on many guises, including its most noisome form, the human head. At one site in northern Brigantia, two wells at Carrawburgh, Northumbria yielded many votive goods, including human skulls and several metal objects as well as heads carved in bronze. These lend further weight to the theory that a sacrificial head cult was prevalent throughout the northern territory of the Brigantes.

In the mid-1960s a surprising number of sinister carved stone heads began turning up throughout the West Riding of Yorkshire. These included free-standing examples as well as those incorporated into the masonry of buildings, either as decoration or more likely, to fend off the evil eye. One of the most interesting was found in Calderdale, set high in the gable end of Mytholmroyd Farm in the village centre. Many more were brought to the attention of the late Sydney Jackson, former curator of the Cartwright Hall Archaeological Group in Bradford. In 1967, Mr Jackson arranged a display of examples collected from all around the West Riding. By this time, heads had been turning up at locations as far apart as Boston Spa, Halifax, Pickering, Wakefield, Mirfield and Skipton.

Such an evocative collection lent further weight to the idea that a head cult in Celtic times was intermingled with a water cult involving rivers, springs and well deities. At Giggleswick the proximity of the church to the three former holy wells suggests (Phillips) a possible link between these sites and the church. Moreover, the widespread existence of pre-Christian pagan shrines concurrent with the earliest foundation of these churches is also postulated.

At Coniston Cold, there is a head built into a road-side barn at the western end of the village, not more than a few yards from the site of a former well. Near Glusburn at Well Head Farm yet another head, fashioned from sandstone, was found embedded in the wall of an outbuilding, and again a spring existed nearby from which the head may have originated, having been cast there by way of libation, or possibly having formed a part of the masonry of a shrine long since demolished.

Apart from the heads already mentioned, others can be seen built into the fabric of the church of St Michael the Archangel at Kirkby Malham. There are two examples within the nave and a third located in the porch. Only 400 yards to the west of Kirkby Malham is the Spa Well located on the north bank of Kirkby Beck. Inside the ancient church at Ledsham, in the very heart of the Celtic kingdom of Elmet, is another head, though broken, forming a corbel at one end of an arch between the nave and the vestry.

Some of these carved heads appear quite definitely ancient as with the Giggleswick examples, others meanwhile have a more recent feel about them. None of the heads however, came from a context that could be dated, so the sceptics argue that, coupled with the numbers found, this brings into doubt the whole issue of their authenticity.

Plate 17: A stone head, built into the north wall of the nave at St. Alkelda's church, Giggleswick. It is believed to have been used in a local Celtic head cult.

Mr Jackson believed that most of the heads were Celtic in origin for no other reason than they shared similar features with others discovered in Ireland and Scotland, and which have been dated by Dr Anne Ross, a leading historian on Celtic culture. For instance, all the finds shared one unusual unifying feature – the cold stare of the almond-shaped, apparently lidless 'Celtic Eye'.

That some heads may be modern suggests (Ross), that the Celtic head cult has continued over a longer period than had originally been thought. The fact that genuine Celtic heads exist at all is an indication that a time had dawned when some wiseman, a Druid perhaps, began to realise that the disposal of human remains in wells was not conducive to maintaining a healthy water supply. Rather than abandon an age-old custom, a substitute head had to be found.

Yorkshire is especially rich in former Holy wells, Hope in 1893 listing almost seventy sites. This is hardly surprising since Brigantia would herself seem to have been the mother goddess of the race calling themselves the Brigantes. They looked to this figure for vitality, fertility and a reliable supply of fresh water. It seems reasonable to believe that many wells in the Pennine region would originally have been dedicated to Brigantia. Perhaps the Bankwell figurine was a fertility offering or even represented the goddess Brigantia herself?

*   *   *

Well worship is one facet of the Celtic culture that remains with us to this day in some areas of the north, thankfully no longer involving head-hunting! In the last century, votive offerings took the form of throwing bent pins into the wells, and more recently coins are still cast into so-called wishing wells before making the customary wish. This reflects the Celtic custom, when functionaries sought from the water goddess some token of the future. We have already mentioned the need for secrecy in the Druid order, and anyone who has sought to influence the future with a visit to a well, knows that for the wish to work it must not become common knowledge.

Wells were sometimes 'dressed' by tying strips of coloured cloth or garlands of flowers to nearby bushes and shrubs. This has taken place at a few sites in Yorkshire within living memory, notably the former St Helen's Well (Rag Well) at Newton Kyme (SE453456), near to the

Rudgate, an ancient crossing point over the river Wharfe. Moreover, elaborate well 'dressing' ceremonies still take place with great pomp each year in some Derbyshire villages, notably Tideswell and Eyam.

Although the Romano-British years saw further uprisings by the native tribes, the period was to remain mostly one of peaceful prosperity and rural development. York continued to thrive as a centre for trade. Along the roads leading into Roman Eboracum wains and pack ponies came and went, loaded with all manner of commodities. Apart from agriculture, the Romans also exploited deposits of lead from the Greenhow area and northern dales, and were working alum and jet deposits from the east coast regions. Potteries were established and iron smelting took place at various localities.

There is little remaining evidence of these activities, due mainly the intensive re-working of the same sites over the centuries that followed Roman withdrawal. Slag has been unearthed at several sites throughout the North York Moors region while at Greenhow the Jackass Level, located not far from the Miners' Arms pub is reputed to have been worked for lead by Celts enslaved by the Romans.

With the retreat from Scotland, many soldiers were finding increasing leisure time to enjoy hunting sports, the forests and moors being alive with venison, wolf and boar. At the same time, many villas were extensively rebuilt, as in the case of Beadlam in the east of our area, including work that could justly be claimed as the very first barn conversion! Unease must have stalked the peaceful Romano-British countryside however, for during the reign of Constantine it had been considered necessary to strengthen the fortifications at York. Some smaller forts were also upgraded, Elslack in particular.

The existence of semi-permanent military camps may suggest a policy of continual military exercises and retraining. But after the evacuation of the north, work would have had to be found for otherwise idle legionaries. Temporary camps may have provided the solution, a sort of community labour programme. One camp at Mastiles Lane (SD915645) in the Yorkshire Dales north of Malham, was discovered in 1957, and may have been an exercise carried out by soldiers based at Elslack. Others camps exist but are not readily visible on the ground. Given a favourable sun angle, the mastiles site can best be viewed from Seaty Hill (SD907654) near Street Gate.

The best-preserved Roman camps can be seen on Cawthorne Moor (SE782900) in the North York Moors north of Malton. The 42 hectare site, including a Bronze Age tumulus, has three military camps and one possible fort, all of which are in an excellent state of preservation. The camps are believed to date from c.AD 100 and were constructed on manoeuvres by the 9th Legion out of York. In the 1920s and 1930s the site was the subject of a major investigation by Professor Ian Richmond, whose work found evidence of internal turf windbreaks in the lee of which the legionaries must have pitched their tents. These features are believed to be unique within the Roman Empire.

Plate 18: Roman camps at Cawthorne, North York Moors. Wade's Causeway, a Roman road extending northwards from Derventio (Malton), cuts across the camp (camp D) on the left of the picture. In the centre the medieval Portergate takes a diagonal line. *(Cambridge University Collection: copyright reserved)*

When visiting Cawthorne, bear in mind that the earthworks are almost 2000 years old; it is, therefore, all the more remarkable that ground features have survived in such detail. The ramparts and ditches appear almost as clear-cut as the day they were built, likewise the detail of the gates. Wade's Causeway can be traced crossing the left-hand camp, while a medieval road known as the Portergate cuts obliquely across the site from south-west to north-east and passes through the gates of the central camp, known as camp C.

In 1975, little of this outstanding monument would have been obvious since the area was suffering from extensive woodland regeneration and scrub. Also, some permanent damage caused by the site being used for wartime mortar training can never be rectified. However, a management plan by the North York Moors National Park will ensure that further damage by arboreal root growth will be halted. This nationally-important site will be protected for future generations, enhanced by the provision of visitor interpretation centres.

In the period between AD 367 to 369 a gradual deterioration of Rome's north-western colony began. Pictish barbarian hordes raiding from beyond Hadrian's Wall, and attacks by Germanic pirates of increasing frequency along the eastern seaboard were the prelude to events that marked the beginning of the end for the Romans in Britain.

We know that beacon fires and smoke were employed by the Romans to draw attention, and that they were familiar with a wooden signalling device not unlike the modern semaphore. Ingleborough Hill (SD743745) derives its name from the Old English *ingle*, meaning fire and *burh* a fortified place. Following the defeat of Venutios, the Romans are known to have lit beacon fires on its summit plateau.

Following a successful, if limited, offensive by Anglo-Saxon barbarians the Romans constructed a chain of fortified signal stations along the east coast (Fig. 11) to provide early warning of further attacks. These beacons stretched between Flamborough Head and Teesside and were built to offer some peace of mind to the occupants of the many villa farms and Romano-British civilian settlements along the fertile coastal fringes of the region. In Yorkshire, these look-out posts were at Whitby, Filey, Ravenscar, Huntcliff, Goldsborough and Scarborough. Of these only the last three sites present remains worthy of inspection.

At Goldsborough (NZ835151) the foundations of the battlemented inner wall are visible, but the visitor to the Huntcliff (NZ687219) site will be disappointed to discover only a few denuded earthworks as reminder of the final crumbling years of Roman rule. One of the most interesting signal stations is at Scarborough where the remains of the Roman structure are located within the outer bailey of the later Norman Castle (TA053893) and consequently are well-preserved.

Plate 19: Roman signal station at Scarborough, located within the outer bailey of a later Norman castle. About a third of the site has been lost to cliff erosion. *(Cambridge University Collection: copyright reserved)*

It stands boldly on the headland separating the south and north bays, the outline of its outer defensive ditch and bank clearly seen, with the foundations of what was once a battlemented inner keep with angle towers. The latter on the seaward side, together with the perimeter earthworks, has been lost over the intervening years due to the retreat of the cliff face. The remainder is clearly visible on the ground, as is the outline of the signal station cum blockhouse and several courses of walling forming part of the gate-house.

Although the discovery of Roman remains at Whitby Abbey (NZ193112) and Raven Hill (NZ980014) near Ravenscar, may be circumstantial proof of the existence of look-out posts at these sites, the exact location of other coastal stations is to some degree conjecture. That roads must have linked these sites with each other and with inland centres such as Malton, perhaps even York, is clear enough; but what is not so obvious is the course they took. This therefore adds a further dimension to the difficulties of determining with any accuracy the location of coastal stations.

One Roman road that impresses with its wild setting is the so-called Wade's Causeway cutting across the North York Moors National Park at Wheeldale Moor. It is an utterly practical route the sole function of which must have been the movement of essential military traffic and personnel. It may be the northward continuation of an important road extending to Malton from York. Although it has not been determined with any reliability, its ultimate destination was probably the signal station at Goldsborough.

The best-preserved section of Wade's Causeway is now under the watchful eye of a warden on behalf of the Department of the Environment. It is classified as a monument of national importance, though yet again the contempt which past Governments have demonstrated is reflected in the extensive damage wreaked on the area when employed as a tank training range! Though it is the first Roman road to receive monument status, the route over Blackstone Edge is in many ways far more worthy of the distinction.

Access to Wheeldale Moor is unrestricted and the road best approached either from Goathland or Stape near Pickering. Choose a day when turbulent clouds are riding the winds and walk the road between Tranmire Bogs (SE803972), along the eastern side of Wheeldale Moor, to where its course changes (SE808981) 200 yards west of Skivick Crag. The atmospherics on such a day will lend an air of drama to the scene as the road strikes with determination over heath and moor. It is easy to visualise the regular traffic that must have plied the road, not only mule trains and wains transporting industrial raw materials, jet and such like, but also a thriving trade in fresh seafoods to inland centres such as Malton and York.

Wade's Causeway was rescued from its suffocating mantle of ling and crowberry between 1914 and 1921. These days, cleaned and renovated, the road displays the foundations of a slightly raised agger some six feet in width for three-quarters of a mile. Apart from the long since eroded surface all other essential features of a Roman road can be seen, including kerbstones, drainage ditches and culverts.

Who was Wade? Tradition tells us that he was a Saxon chieftain living at Mulgrave and accredited with the killing of the sadistic King Ethelred in the year 794. Four years afterwards, Wade himself was mortally wounded by one of Ethelred's successors but managed to flee back to Mulgrave, where he died. Close to East Barnby is Wade's Stone (NZ831130) and a mile away at Goldsborough (NZ831143) a similar one; both are said to mark his final resting place.

Putting history aside, legend informs us that a local giant named Wada and his wife Bel, were responsible for the road. They were engaged in the building of the castles at Mulgrave (NZ839117) and Pickering (NZ799846). Working on a castle each, they shared a gigantic hammer which they hurled to each other across the intervening eighteen miles of moorland. According to local folklore, Wada constructed the causeway to link the two places.

Today, the only mystery surrounding Wade's Causeway concerns its destination beyond the camps at Cawthorne. Until recently, nothing was certain. We are still not entirely sure of its line north of the preserved section, but it may have passed close to a farm (NZ814009) at Julian Park where a stone was unearthed bearing a Latin inscription. The alignment can be traced where it appears in woods (NZ811026), slightly north of here. A feasible course would have been along Lease Rigg and then down to a ford over the Esk at Grosmont.

The general picture of Roman Yorkshire began fitting together with greater clarity after excavation at Lease Rigg led to a recognition of the earthwork here as a Roman fort. This is just visible either side of the moor road (NZ815042) to Grosmont two hundred yards north-east of a farm at High Burrows. Excavations showed that the fort possessed a granary and initially consisted of a timber and turf palisade built in the 2nd century AD.

The identification of Lease Rigg as a permanent Roman fort goes some way toward explaining the existence of the camps at Cawthorne, yet poses more questions than it answers. Its food storage facilities were small, and could hardly have been adequate to provision the smallest of infantry units. This would suggest that part of the garrison was billeted elsewhere, though the question is where. If Lease Rigg was a permanent fort, it was more than the usual day's march from the nearest known fort, at Malton. As has previously been suggested, one of the Cawthorne camps may have been a permanent fort. If correct, it provides a vital piece in the jigsaw but still leaves unresolved the final terminus of Wade's Causeway.

Toward the close of the 4th century, a rumour of unease was in the

air, driven across The Wolds as dark clouds gathered on the eastern
horizon like harbingers of impending doom. Appearing suddenly out
of a North Sea mist, Anglian pirates hauled their craft up onto the
eastern beaches. The cry would go up: fear, fire, foe! Beacon fires
would be torched up and down the coast, in a chain reaction spreading the word of despair. From signal station to station the alarm would
finally reach Malton or York where garrisons could be mobilised. But
it was already too late, the writing was on the wall. Rome's most
distant frontier was by then crumbling beyond recovery.

It is not unreasonable to assume that the network of look-out
stations built to warn the Romans of attack from the sea probably
continued down the Holderness coast as far as Spurn Point. Unfortunately the coastline here is formed of soft marls and the dark grey
Kimmeridge Clays which offer little if any resistance to the erosive
might of the North Sea. The coastline we know has changed beyond
recognition down the centuries and any possible clues to the location
of Roman structures have long since been lost to the sea.

Coastal erosion has been a matter for study since the early 18th
century, when accurate measurements were first recorded. In a
paper[13] published in the last century by Canon Isaac Taylor, a
calculated estimate for coastal erosion was given for the coastline
between Spurn Head and Bridlington. Based on the assumption that
erosion rates had remained constant between his chosen datum
points, he suggested a mean retreat of seven feet per annum. This
suggested that over thirty-five square miles of land had been swal-
lowed by the sea between 1086 and 1800 (see Fig. 15). If this was
correct, it is not surprising that there are no surviving remains of
Roman signal stations along this stretch of the Yorkshire seaboard.
Given that the rate of retreat has been consistent, the coastline of this
part of Yorkshire at the time of the Roman withdrawal would have
been two and a half miles out in the North Sea!

The knowledge that a signal station existed at Flamborough is
supported by the existence of a Roman road travelling east towards
Bridlington. Alternatively the Romans could have had a port at the
latter location. The alignment of the Roman road is taken up by the
course of a modern road from Stamford Bridge to Fridaythorpe via

---

13
  The Ploughland and the Plough

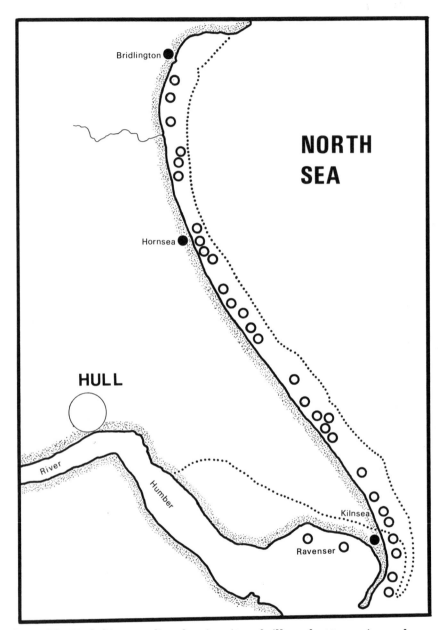

Fig. 15: The Yorkshire coastline showing sites of villages lost to erosion and a shifting coastline.

Garrowby Hill. Today it is automobiles and not carts that trace the A64 as it climbs the steep Wolds escarpment.

After Fridaythorpe, the eastward continuation is less apparent but one possible route went by way of Fimber (SE895605) and Life Hill (SE931619). This conjectured alignment is picked up again at the cross-roads (TA008642) by Kilham West Field, from where it proceeds via West End, Kilham and as a minor country lane called Wold Gate. As such, the road passes Rudston Beacon (TA095656) and Fish Pond Woods (TA145673) slightly south of Boynton Hall, henceforth one assumes, to the headland at Flamborough.

Curtain call on 4th century Roman Britain was hastened by raiding Teutons who arrived in ever-increasing numbers, despite the provision of early warning stations. In 367, an alliance of northern heathens was rapidly bringing Britain to its knees, but problems for the Romans were not confined to the west side of the channel; similar raids by multitudes of Saxons were occurring along the Rhine in the year 370. Thirteen years later Hadrian's Wall was breached in several places and the Picts poured their hordes south, raiding deep into Brigantia. In the year 387 and again from 407 onwards, Magnus Maximus and Constantine III each respectively withdrew troops across the channel to counter uprisings in Gaul. These actions simply hastened the end of Roman authority in Britain.

By 393, growing problems in Gaul coupled with a widespread mutiny among the rank and file legionaries had written the final chapter of the Pax Romana. By the year 407, Rome itself was crumbling and those who still maintained allegiance to the military state withdrew across the channel into Gaul.

Thus, a sadly-depleted and harried force represented the last remnant of Roman rule, yet the loss of Britain was barely noticed. Rome itself was beheaded and its leaders scurrying about like headless chickens in the face of the gathering uprising. When it received a request from the Britons for military assistance in repelling barbarians, it was unable to or incapable of sparing either money or manpower. In 410, Flavius Honorius advised the inhabitants of British towns that they were on their own and so ended almost 400 years of Roman occupation.

5

Territorial Imperative

Men come and go and that is all of history
– Joaquin Miller.

The long and strife-torn centuries between the Roman exodus and
the **norman conquest**, a period frequently called the **dark ages**, were
years of fearful upheaval for Yorkshire, and for the country as a
whole. During the 5th century British soil was invaded by many
Germanic races originating from around the North Sea coast. These
people came from the Jutland peninsula and the islands of Fresia
north of the Rhine estuary, but were mostly of the Saxones and Angli
races inhabiting the lands between the Baltic and the river Ems.

Historians of later periods often referred to these races collectively
as Anglo-Saxons, usually drawing little if any cultural distinctions,
though they included the Jutes and other lesser tribal groups. Indeed
by the 8th century the terms Angle and Saxon were interchangeable
in common parlance, even among Anglo-Saxons when utilised to
describe themselves.

Why the Dark Ages? The very term conjures up a vision – or rather
a lack of vision – for this slice of history, when nothing could be
further from the truth. Some details concerning the six and a half
centuries leading to the Norman Conquest remain sketchy and uncertain, especially for the years immediately after the first Danish
raids. This is not quite so surprising considering that at this time the
church represented more than simply religion; it was synonymous
with knowledge and education. It is for this reason that the earliest
records generally came from monastic scholars. It followed too, that

with the Viking destruction of religious centres, the gentle stroking of quill on parchment fell silent.

One of the most valuable records of this period was that produced by the Venerable Bede. He was born c.673 near the monastery at Wearmouth and went on to receive a religious education, becoming a monk and later a priest, scribe and teacher. He was without doubt one of the most influential characters of his day and may justly be regarded as the country's very first historian, though his work was mostly concerned with religious matters. He produced *The Ecclesiastical History of the English People*, a valuable document from which we glean a great deal about life in the Dark Ages.

*   *   *

In previous chapters we have seen how cultures from the Neolithic to the Iron Age left their own distinctive mark on the countryside. Barrows and megalithic monuments survived as a reminder of the Stone and Bronze Age periods, similarly the hill forts and military roads reflected the aspirations and insecurities of the Celts and Romans who came later. Yet it was the Angles, and the Scandinavians following in their wake who made the greatest impact on the landscape and social structure of what we now call Yorkshire.

Out of these chaotic centuries emerged the greatest single facet of present-day rural English life, the country village we take so much for granted. Christianity too, though it endured frequent incursions of paganism and suffered the attention of a succession of iconoclasts, eventually emerged the stronger for it. This is reflected today in country parishes, many of which correspond almost to the old manorial limits imposed during the Viking annexations of the 9th and 10th centuries.

However, the notion of national unity, that is an England ruled by and for the English, was an ideal which was to have a long gestation period: over four hundred years, during which the intervening centuries witnessed much bloodshed. The story of how Roman Britain evolved through several dynastic kingdoms to become Anglo-Saxon England, and drawing a parallel, how Brigantia finally emerged as the county of Yorkshire, is an extremely convoluted one.

The Dark Ages was a volatile period and poses many questions for which the answers may never be fully known. Much of the history of these years appears only in documents isolated from the events by several generations of oral tradition. It follows that chroniclers of those times would have access to details that would be subject to change, distortion and heresy. As we shall see, there were many historical pawns along the hazardous road to political stability, nonetheless each represented an important milestone on our long journey to shire identity.

One of the first things to happen as the chill winds of change whistled across that uncertain land was a widespread abandonment. The whole of the East Riding of Yorkshire had developed into a prosperous farming region, but it began slipping into wholesale decay. The Roman northern command, based at York, had placed great demands on the surrounding countryside for staples such as cereals and other commodities. One can imagine the scene after they left – acres of corn and other crops ripening in the sun, but left unharvested to wither on the stem and to be choked by the return of wild grasses.

The land everywhere surrendered to the opportunist plants of the wild heaths, the people in their turn falling foul of the heathen bands out of the east and north. All the evidence gathered from pollen sampling suggests that a regeneration of natural woodland took place where in the Iron Age open farmland had flourished. This was especially so in some areas of the North York Moors, where even after the Norman Conquest peasants were still felling woods that had become established and matured during the Dark Ages.

> From heaven unto that field is born the seed
> Of nourishment, which brings forth generous sheaves
> A thousandfold. Alas, that such a crop,
> A holy harvest, falls before grim war.

The Brigantes in Yorkshire had long since forsaken their traditional settlements of the highland zones, in favour of the more sedentary existence that went with the Roman agricultural lifestyle. Faced with economic decline as the system collapsed which had provided the political stability for growth, the more powerful Britons would have attempted to retain some measure of control, eager to preserve the status quo. Alas that pestilence and plague were to become efficient allies of agricultural decline to the extent that the native population too sank into a desperate, impoverished state.

It is easy to imagine the tattered remnants of the Celtic people rallying about any leader that could offer them direction or hope. And it would seem probable that this is what happened, for eventually they gathered themselves into smaller autonomous units, kingdoms as it were. It was this trend that eventually was to separate the Celtic race into the Welsh Celts, the Celts of the south-west and the British. Like the phoenix rising from the ashes, out of the 'free-for-all' that remained after the end of Roman rule, emerged the British principality of Elmet, a nucleus of Celtic cultural unity.

Though the full extent of this kingdom is uncertain, it is believed to have endured well into the 7th century and was centred upon the lower reaches of both the Calder and Aire valleys (Fig. 16). Sherburn-in-Elmet, Barwick-in-Elmet and Leeds (Loidis), a possible capital, are place-names surviving to the present day which give some idea of the territorial range. Another nucleus of British influence seems to have been Rheged in the north. This stretched around the Solway Firth down through Cumbria, with its southern boundary extending into Yorkshire at Mallerstang and the head-waters of both the Swale and the Ure.

As Saxon raids became ever more frequent, Celtic leaders entered into nebulous agreements with foreign mercenaries to help them stave off their foes. According to the Anglo-Saxon Chronicle for the year 443 the Britons sent messengers to Rome begging military assistance to help them fight the Welsh of Strathclyde. The request fell on deaf ears since any possible help was diverted to a war with the Huns.

Sometime during the mid-5th century, a shadowy figure called Vortigern made his appearance. Little is known about this man and his deeds, nor exactly when he lived. However, he seems to have been a person of some standing whom Gildas called a 'proud tyrant' and whom Bede later called a king. Vortigern is accredited with inviting Germanic mercenaries to help organise resistance against the northern barbarians. The two brothers Hengist and Horsa are said to have come to Britain in this way.

The very first settlement of Germanic peoples in our region, is

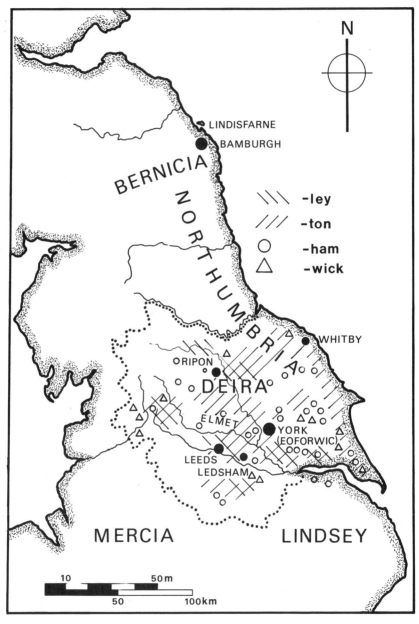

Fig. 16: Yorkshire in the Dark Ages showing the relative distribution of Anglo-Saxon place-name components.

thought to have taken place sometime during the closing years of the 4th century, after soldiers were recruited by the Roman administration to bolster Britain's defences against attack by other barbarians.

Although in Anglo-Saxon tradition Hengist is remembered as the first Jutish king of Kent, as a historical character he remains obscure. Some scholars doubt the existence of these two brothers, whose names translate from the Old English as gelding and horse. Bede himself gave account of their ancestry, tracing them four centuries back to the pagan god Woden. This story clearly has its roots firmly planted in mythical tradition, which states that several Anglo-Saxon dynastic families also trace their ancestry to the same deity. For this reason one must remain sceptical about the existence of Hengist and Horsa.

In the event, the Anglo-Saxon Chronicle records in the entry for 455 AD that Hengest and Horsa revolted against Vortigern and, after calling on reinforcements, ended up fighting the Britons they had been invited to help. Thus we see how Vortigern had inadvertently acted as the catalyst that was to precipitate further and greater ruin on the Britons.

*   *   *

It was clearly a turbulent episode, the Dark Ages yes, but one which was punctuated by a long roll-call of aspirant dynastic leaders, war-lords and church men, the likes of Edwin, Oswy, Ida, Paulinus, Swein Forkbeard, Cnut, Harold Godwinsson, and many other important figures who would shape history. It was also the age of Arthur, for sometime toward the middle of the 5th century this popular personage of fame and legend takes up his place in our historical traditions.

The notion of King Arthur and his squeaky clean Knights of the Round Table, emerged as one of the great European traditions, but it remains pure fabrication. Though the original source of the story is vague, it seems probable that it appeared in Celtic times. Later, the Norman romantics seized upon the flimsiest shred of fact and wove into it tales of chivalrous knights and great deeds. It was they who saw Arthur, their champion, as a ruler who meted out justice from his court of Camelot, while seated at a round table surrounded by the likes of Sir Galahad and Lancelot of the Lake.

Just as later writers with a liberal application of poetic licence made Dick Turpin ride all the way from London to York within daylight, Geoffrey of Monmouth in his glowing 12th century chicanery[14] created the courageous battle leader who fought alongside the Britons to conquer their Saxon oppressors, but who himself was not above subduing vast areas of Europe. If we sift through all this literary nonsense we might suspect that there is some basis of fact to the legend. But are we being seduced by a quixotic tale? Though we may never learn the true identity of Arthur, his place in our heritage is assured.

For our sources of Arthurian history, albeit lacking concrete evidence, we have the texts of Gildas, the venerable Bede, and Nennius, a Welsh ecclesiastic who lived in the 9th century. These writings were committed to parchment long after the events and make only cursory reference to the reign of Arthur. Though these works may be tainted with half truths and distorted by the inadequacies of oral tradition, they hint of decisive battles from which eventually emerged the independent nations of England, Wales and Scotland.

Arthur remains obscure and shrouded in the mists of time, yet it seems possible that he was a descendant, perhaps the son of a Romanised Briton who had inherited the tactical skills and battle strategies of the Romans. Contemporary writers soon after the so-called Age of Arthur ended, and before the legends had time to cloud the issue, tell of a man who in his short reign as 'king' achieved fame as a great military commander. They remember also, the few remaining lowland armies of the 7th century, referring to them as 'Arthur's Heirs'.

In Yorkshire, there existed the kingdom of Elmet. Perhaps through the Arthurian tales we, as beneficiaries of the distant past, are being treated to a vague glimpse of a mystic warrior who was called Artorius, and who seemingly headed a highly mobile and successful army based at Elmet.

14
  Historia Regum Britanniae

The problem of identifying Arthur does not rest with lack of information. Quite the contrary, for the facts are there, but in the intervening centuries they have become confused, changed and suspect. One could compare the details of these years to that of a reference library in which some mischievous person has ransacked the books, erased all the titles and page numbers and mixed them all up. The historical evidence is uncollated, tenuous and as a result difficult to arrange in a correct chronology.

Attempts to pin a true identity on the legendary Arthur, are as problematic as they are with Hengist, Horsa and a handful of other vague characters of the Dark Ages. Any aspiration to find the sphere of his influence would take the historian the full length and breadth of Britain. There is hardly a county that does not lay some claim to Arthur, however tenuous. His birthplace is said to be Tintagel Castle in Cornwall, while there is an Arthur's Seat in Edinburgh and an Arthur's Round Table near Penrith in Cumbria.

Though the stories and the myths relating his deeds linger still, even a mighty warrior such as Arthur could not endure indefinitely, and perhaps he fought his last battle, courageously, and in the words of Tennyson amid:

> Shocks, and the splintering spear, the hard mail hewn,
> Shield-breakings, and the clash of brands, the crash
> Of battleaxes on shattered helms, and shrieks.

This time, the traditional and seemingly universal theme of Arthur reflects a woebegone tale of treachery, death and subsequent despair, in which the people of a later age lament the end, through perfidy, of a good and just ruler who sallied forth for the cause of the Briton. His final resting place? Tradition has it that Arthur is interred at Glastonbury Abbey.

Elevating the meagre historical evidence into a folk tale, Sir Thomas Malory[15] in the 15th century saw 'his' Arthur, king and good natured saviour of his subjects, not as having passed away, but merely suspended in a deep sleep, until such a time when, in the nation's

---

15
    author of *Le Morte d'Arthur*

hour of greatest need, he shall be awakened and again ride forth onto the battlefield in defence of those in distress.

Because of this widespread belief, folk tradition provides that Arthur and his Knights, resplendent in shining armour, slumber till that day of reckoning beneath features of the British landscape up and down the country. In Yorkshire, he sleeps beneath Castle Hill (SE152141) in the West Riding and also under Freeborough Hill (NZ690127) on the North York Moors. The valleys of Swaledale and Mallerstang also have their Arthurian associations, claiming Pendragon Castle (NZ783027) as Arthur's birthplace, as son of Uther Pendragon, in the former forest of Rheged which flourished in those parts.

Tracing the River Swale further down dale brings us to the delightful market town of Richmond (NZ170010). If any location merits a place in the legend, surely Richmond is second to none. The historic town is dominated by its superb Norman castle whose bailey forms an equilateral triangle perched high above the river. Once again we find the recurring theme of the sleeping monarch biding his time until the call to arms. The tradition is echoed in the familiar tales of lost caverns and secret vaults deep beneath the castle. Beside the slumbering army, it is said, lies the sword Excalibur and a hunting horn with which to arouse the king should any brave soul find his way into the secret chamber.

There is a most enchanting local legend concerning one Potter Thompson, a none-too-bright resident who found the entrance to Arthur's vault. He was one of those timid, hen-pecked souls who could never do anything right for his wife. One day, despondent as ever, he wandered down by the river at the base of the fort, and there to his utter astonishment found a small passageway partially hidden by boulders. The discovery was all the more remarkable for he had often covered the same ground and never seen the subterranean opening leading into the underworld.

Though he had never been a particularly brave man his curiosity soon gained the upper hand. Advancing cautiously into the cave he followed a devious route down into the limestone. At length he emerged into a large chamber washed with a peculiar glow. In the half light, he saw the band of knights laid out in full battle dress, their swords nearby and their heads rested on their shields as pillows. One of the warriors he noted wore a crown of bright gold but even this treasure was dulled by comparison to the sight which next met his gaze.

In the centre of the hall he espied a stone slab on which was laid out a horn of gold and a mighty sword contained in a jewel-encrusted sheath. Wishing to return with this as proof of what he had found, he attempted to remove the weapon from its scabbard, but each movement was accompanied by a corresponding stirring of the knights. The more he drew the sword, the more the clattering of their armour terrified him so that, with nerves at breaking point, he turned on his heels for the exit.

He ran, and ran, and as he did so a mysterious wind gathered, sweeping poor Thompson off his feet and up the tunnel back to the surface, all the while an eery voice could be heard chanting:

> Potter Thompson, Potter Thompson,
> If thou hadst either drawn
> The sword or wound the horn,
> Thou hadst been the luckiest man
> That ever yet was born.

From that day on, he roamed the streets and wynds of Richmond town vowing that if he rediscovered the secret gallery he would blow the horn, and draw the great sword, but alas he never did find the passage again.

And what of Arthur's famed court of Camelot? Tourists are told that Cadbury Castle in Somerset is where he held judgement over the land. In Yorkshire, Castle Hill (SE152141) at Almondbury near Huddersfield is suggested. If Arthur was a battle leader of the Celts in Yorkshire during the 5th century, Camelot may well have been at Almondbury which we already know had been an important Brigantian stronghold.

Texts from the 2nd century provide tenuous clues through place-names which may be Romanised versions of earlier Celtic form. Ptolemy's *Geography* and the *Notitia Dignitatum* and later *Itinera* of Antoninus Pius mentions two northern forts, namely Cambodunum and Camulodunum. Their locations are vague to say the least. A crude map of Britain produced by Ptolemy is little help as the coastline bears no resemblance to today's charts and therefore cannot be used as a datum. Moreover, the Romans had no means of accurately measuring the passage of time, a prerequisite for determining angles of longitude.

There is some confusion regarding possible locations for these forts. Camulodunum appears to be vested in the area between the city of Bradford and Standedge on the county boundary with Greater Manchester. Slack is believed to be a likely site or Castleshaw close to a Roman military highway which crossed over the Pennine hills from Tadcaster to Manchester. Cambodunum is thought to have been somewhere near Cleckheaton, but whether Camelot was a later corruption of either of these names we may never know. I would go as far as saying there is every chance that it was. Perhaps, after all, we can ascribe the very centre of Arthurian folk tradition right here in the West Riding of Yorkshire.

From a purely romantic standpoint, I prefer to believe that Castle Hill was the focus of Arthurian legend, simply because it is the only location that comes anywhere near matching the grand setting one would expect of such an illustrious gathering. Wether Arthur, Artorius or whoever he was, held court at Castle Hill and planned the defence of the Britons against the Saxons, we cannot say. In either event it proved impossible of the Celts to stem the rising tide of the English for long.

*   *   *

As we pare away the years of the 5th century, we find the barbarians infiltrating from the north and east became more numerous; not simply the few Picts and scattered Saxon brigands that had contributed to the downfall of Rome's most distant province, but more determined waves of Teutonic pirates, the culturally-related Angles and Jutes. After many subservient generations under the Roman yoke the once proud and warlike Celts had by this time lost the knowledge or the will to fight. They were, in effect, adrift in a rudderless boat in a sea of enemies.

It is tempting to speculate on the outcome for Yorkshire, indeed Britain as a whole, had the Romans not overstretched their Empire. The Romans were great civil engineers and left behind an excellent integrated network of roads. Construction was suspended when they departed, though as we shall see in the next chapter later monarchs found the existing roads of strategic benefit.

The Romano-British years also produced vast quantities of Samian ware, a fine pottery, well-fired and much of it magnificently ornate. Again after the Roman exodus we find none of this. Flung once again into the turmoil of simply surviving, the Romanised Britons no longer had the time or the inclination to devote to such crafts. Although roads proved of continuing benefit in the post-Roman period, the grandeur of their towns sank into oblivion. Even mighty Eboracum crumbled, albeit not entirely ruinous, for the colonnades of what had been the Roman *principia* were still to be seen, four centuries after it had been deserted.

In the year 527, a religious mission under Augustine arrived in southern England bearing the proclamation of Rome, a message which in the event would take thirty years to arrive in the north. By that time the pagans had gained a firm foothold along the eastern seaboard.

Though we can feel certain there was no overnight slaughter by these new overlords, there are however few clues to the precarious stance of the Britons at this time. Our lack of understanding of this period is exacerbated by a devastating plague that ravaged Britain around 540. Another contributory factor was the lack of literacy that came with the pagan English. The middle of the 6th century witnessed divisions among the surviving northern British clans, with the Celtic enclave of Elmet rising to supremacy. The English had begun working their way inland and further south in the Midlands they founded Mercia.

Although the Anglo-Saxons were a racial minority compared with the indigenous Briton, during the following five centuries they were to exact sweeping changes. What we now call York grew into Eoforwik (the town of the boar), an important Anglo-Saxon commercial centre trading throughout northern Europe. It was they who eventually established a unified culture in a country which would later be referred to as England. With it went a coinage, a quite sophisticated fiscal system, and a standardised tongue (Englisc) which in time was to give to the world its most widely spoken language.

Despite these cultural advances it was a capricious period from which emerge precious few clues to its passing. There is however, one enduring bequest to these turbulent years, as a mere glance at street signs and modern maps of the county will at once reveal. The Dark Ages live on today in the widespread distribution of Anglo-Saxon and Scandinavian place-names. These not only give a hint of what the countryside was like at the time our distant ancestors were putting down their roots, but provide valuable evidence from which the historian can deduce possible migration routes.

The analysis of pollen grains taken from peat deposits tell us that the lowest regions of the valleys were covered with willow marsh and alder scrubland. By contrast, the higher ground of the North York Moors and Pennines, the rolling chalk hills of The Wolds, the flanks of the dales, together with their tributary gills, supported oak-dominant woodland.

In our region, westward penetration by the Angles was aided by natural waterways such as the Humber. This became the gateway to the valleys of the Ouse and Derwent into what later became the East Riding, and westwards to the West Riding by way of the Don and Calder, river names which despite the intervening centuries preserve some semblance of their Celtic etymology.

Where the Angles cleared away the trees, they established settlements which in their dialect were given names ending with the suffix *-leah*. Today, this is manifested in villages and towns with names ending in *-ley*: Finningley, Wickersley, Helmsley, Bentley, Barnsley, Emley and Yearsley being indicative. Because the native woods grew thickest on the acid soil substrates of the Carboniferous Period, in Yorkshire represented by the millstone grit country and the coal measures, the distribution of *-ley* type names we find, correspond roughly to this type of terrain.

Examples are found in the lowest reaches of the Calder Valley, Airedale, the Wharfe, the coalfields south of Leeds and east of Sheffield, and especially in the Vale of York. In some localities, the Anglo-Saxon settlers took over the management of derelict Romano-Celtic arable farms. There is archaeological material to support this in a few cases, for instance at Roman towns such as Catarotonium.

The availability of reliable fresh water would have been an important controlling factor in settlement. If we consider that ground water in the East Riding comes from depth, contained in the underlying Cretaceous chalk and older Jurassic limestone strata, settlement would from necessity have taken place where water springs to the surface. Strong freshets occur along the south side of the Vale of Pickering, again at the base of the chalk escarpments forming the edge of The Wolds, and where springs form in the many valleys dissecting this rolling landscape.

Early in the 7th century westward migration of the Angles was almost blocked by the British of Elmet until the death of Ceretic in 617. The few *-ley* names we do find deeper into the Pennines probably betray a free pioneering spirit among a few hardy groups successful in pushing through to the west. In Wharfedale, Otley, Ilkley, Farnley and Drebley are one group, Grantley, Ripley, Pately, Bewerly and Darley in Nidderdale another. Bordley near Malham and Wensley in the dale of the same name must represent two more outliers.

By AD 547 the Anglian vestigial kingdom of Bernicia was established and had extended its sphere of interest from the latitude of the Tweed south to the river Tees. The affairs of this embryo English dynasty were administered by King Ida, first of a long line of both pagan and Christian rulers. The seat of power had as its focus Bamburgh Castle, a fort which Ida dedicated to Bebba, his queen.

To begin with, the river Tees formed a natural frontier between Bernicia and Deira, the latter including all of what today is the East Riding of Yorkshire south as far as the Humber. If a tradition perpetuated by Nennius has any credence, frequent running battles between Ida's sons and the Britons would suggest Bernician influence extended very little way inland.

Æthelfrith came to power in the year 593, at a time when the last remnants of the British in Yorkshire were making efforts to secure their cultural destiny. An alliance with their counterparts in Lancashire and North Wales, together with the Picts of Scotland represented a final but futile effort to stem the English advance. Time and tide wait for no man, Celt or otherwise. Under the command of Æthelfrith the English army in Deira was strengthened by forces from further north. This move seems to have resulted, around the year 600, in a decisive battle in the Catterick area, said to have ended with the death of several Celtic leaders.

Deira and Bernicia then merged to become a more powerful Anglo-Saxon territory whose name is derived from the old northern English *Hymrbre*, by which Bede frequently referred to the people living north of the Humber. From this moment onwards the fortunes of the new state of Northumbria are in effect those also of Yorkshire. It was a turbulent period of history and one which promised its main protagonists everything, yet nothing at all; the only guaranteed outcome being death by warfare, disease or treachery.

The pagan warrior Æthelfrith wed the daughter of Aelle, first King of Deira, and hence through a marriage of convenience succeeded in usurping authority over the southern half of the territory. Other members of the Deiran royal dynasty went into exile with the East Angles where King Redwald held sway over all Anglo-Saxons south of Northumbria.

Being a ruler in the Dark Ages was fraught and forever overshadowed by the ever shifting clouds of uncertainty. The short reign of Æthelfrith came to a bloody climax in 616 when he was killed by Redwald somewhere near the east bank of the River Idle at Hatfield Chase near Doncaster. Edwin succeeded him as king of Northumbria, and the next year led his Northumbrian army against Elmet. This well-planned offensive succeeded in overthrowing Ceretic, the last surviving British king.

Just a few miles east of Leeds, near Aberford, some impressive linear earthworks may have had strategic importance for Ceretic in his defence of Elmet from attack by the English (see Fig. 17). From the direction the rampart faces, this would appear to be possible at South Dyke (SE446377), a mile east of Green Hill. However, in the case of a second site, the larger, more impressive dimensions suggest it might have been a frontier defence thrown up by the Northumbrians against Mercian aggression from the south.

From a point (SE409380) about half a mile east of Potterton Bridge, near Barwick-in-Elmet, this massive earthwork stretches east for two miles. Marked on maps as The Ridge and Becca Banks, it runs almost parallel to the north bank of Cock Beck as far as Aberford. Its continuation, The Rein, can be picked up again just beyond the A1 (SE438377) from where it trends south-east for a mile and half in a straight line, ending (SE452366) near Lotherton Hall beside the B1217.

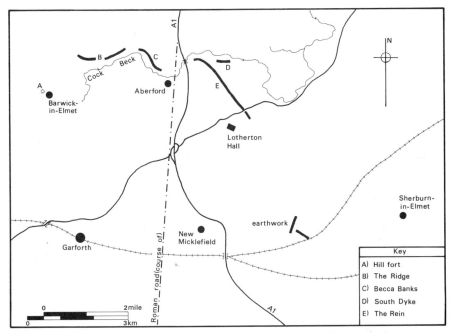

Fig. 17: Defensive earthwork emplacements in the Celtic territory of Elmet: A) Earthwork containing a later Norman motte; B) The Ridge; C) Becca Banks; D) South Dyke; E) The Rein.

Other earthworks in the Elmet area that may be also be late-6th century include the hill fort at Barwick-in-Elmet (SE398375) and another series of trenches in Huddleston Old Wood (SE466335), between Micklefield and Sherburn-in-Elmet. From the extent of these earthworks a major offensive must have been expected, but from which quarter is not certain. Standing upon these ramparts in the very heart of Elmet evokes the gruesome aftermath of the heavy hand to hand combat that must have taken place around these frontier works.

The defeat of the British at Elmet and subsequent toppling of their heathen icons signalled the emergence of English Christianity during the early 7th century. In 619 king Edwin married Æthelburga, a Christian princess from Kent, and a year later was himself converted

Plate 20: Earthworks known as The Rein, situated in the former Celtic territory of Elmet, east of Leeds.

to the faith at Goodmanham in the East Riding. That same year one of Edwin's ministers, Lilla, was killed in a heroic sacrifice near the river Derwent, when he threw himself upon an assassin's blade to protect Edwin. According to tradition Lilla was later buried within a large Bronze Age round barrow on the North York Moors. This is located (SE889987) on Fylingdales Moor within sight of the M.O.D. early warning station (now dismantled). When excavated, the mound revealed jewellery and ornaments of gold and silver.

Edwin was baptised by the missionary Paulinus at York in April of 627, the year in which Lilla is thought to have been honoured with a stone cross built on top of his grave mound. This has since become known as Lilla's Howe and is one of the earliest known Christian monuments. What may be another, late Anglo-Scandinavian tumulus is marked by a mound of gritstone cobbles on the east bank of Kingsdale Beck (SD709787), three and a half miles north of Ingleton.

At some time in the past, the beck has changed its course and is in the process of washing away this scheduled monument.

The Christian mission of Paulinus to Northumberland lasted for about seven years, a fact reflecting the relative stability which came with the victory over the Britons. It was to lend a new impetus to Anglo-Saxon westwards expansion, of which we can gain some idea of the full extent from a second, more significant name component: *-tun*. This appears today throughout the region, in the Dales at Wennington, Horton, Ingleton, Starbotton and Skipton, and in the North York Moors and Wolds with Settrington, Carlton, Sproxton, Sutton, Nunnington, Bridlington and Middleton. South of Leeds we find Royston, Dinnington, Norton, Crofton, Walton and Kirkburton.

The *-ton* element is more widespread than is the case with *-ley* and differs in that, rather than being symptomatic of a nucleus of family groups, it represented the places where a smallholding was founded. Most of the archetypal *-ton* names are confined to the Vale of York and The Wolds where the tilth was richer, unlike the heavily-wooded regions which required greater manpower and resources to clear, cultivate and manage.

Other elements that are diagnostic of Anglian settlement take the form of *-ing* and *-ham* two suffixes individually or when combined, indicating where Anglian farmers cleared more extensive open areas of land. This gave way to the larger village with common grazing. Examples occur in Pickering, Lastingham, Middleham, Feetham, Meltham, Rotherham, Addingham, Manningham and Malham. In South Yorkshire there are only three examples of *-ham*: Rotherham, Bilham Grange and Bilham House Farm.

The place-names cited here are just a few examples that are obvious from a glance at the map, many more being apparent (see Fig. 16). These hamlets or smallholdings established by the first Anglian pioneers would, after several generations eventually evolve into the nucleated village with its well-kept green, so much a feature of the countryside of today.

*   *   *

Although hunting, gathering and trade would still have been an important facet of Anglo-Saxon life, a staple crop would have been a first priority upon putting down roots. To this end, a system of arable fields spread throughout the more fertile valleys. Woodland clearance continued through slash and burn agriculture, or by tree-felling either to create new agricultural plots, or for firewood and building materials. Grazing by sheep and cattle would ensure that natural woodlands never regenerated, these eventually reverting to rough pasture or scrubby heath.

Location of settlements would often take place on river terraces above alluvial marshland which was eventually cultivated as meadow. In the Yorkshire Dales the best ploughland was often on the gentler sloping ground leading back from the terrace, though this presented problems for the team of oxen. It was usual for ploughs to be drawn by teams of oxen working in tandem and it was almost impossible to work across these gradients without the whole contraption slithering downslope and interfering with the lower furrows.

To obviate these difficulties, and to stabilize the land in areas where the soil profile was shallow and rainfall high, the land was farmed in steps, forming a terraced effect up the hillside. Though an Anglo-Saxon innovation, these ploughing strips, or lynchets, were often re-worked or new ones constructed by the Scandinavian farmers who came afterwards. One can gain some impression of what an Anglo-Saxon strip farm was like in the Yorkshire Dales National Park. They can still be seen in upper Wharfedale, Airedale, Wensleydale and along the line of the Craven Fault between Settle and Ingleton.

After several generations of Anglo-Saxon farming practice, the rural landscape took on a form we would recognise today. If we were to be transported backwards in time we would see the traditional nucleated arrangement of dwellings which forms the basis of the modern-day village. Buildings would be erected in groups clustered about a central open area, which later developed into the village green.

By the time the Danes arrived, the pattern of settlement was well-founded, with meadows occupying the valley bottom and ploughland established on the rising ground either side. Somewhere midway would be the village. The wilder fell country and wasteland would serve as rough pasture and also provide the raw materials for thatching. The similarity between the settlements of Angle or Scandinavian today makes it difficult to positively distinguish between a village with Anglo-Saxon roots and one established by the Vikings.

The clearest evidence of lynchets exists in the pastures around Thorpe (SE013617), and from there almost all the way up Wharfedale to Borrans (SD968726), just outside Kettlewell. Others are to be seen at Clapham below Bank Wood (SD744697), a little north of Stainforth (SD821676) and on the east flank of the shallow valley below Malham Cove (SD896634), adjacent to the Romano-Celtic field patterns mentioned in previous chapters.

The common field arrangement for arable, pasture and meadow land that was typical of an Anglian settlement is still visible today around some Yorkshire villages. A drove way, known as the 'outgang' provided a means of driving stock across arable land to or from the pasture. This drove way survives in the green lanes, that wind about rural areas without any apparent sense of purpose. This is reflected further by the country road exhibiting the double right-angled bend separated by a short straight stretch. These occur because the terminus of drove ways leading from two neighbouring villages did not exactly match. Today they often trace the parish boundary.

With the emergence of English Christianity we find the Anglo-Saxons leave more objective evidence of their influence in shaping the Yorkshire we know today. Edwin's baptism took place in a church hurriedly erected specifically for that purpose and it must have been built from timber, as were all early Saxon churches. Unfortunately none of these buildings exist in our area today. The one at Greensted in Essex is a quite remarkable survival of 9th century Anglo-Saxon work, but falls outside the scope of this book.

*   *   *

The pre-Conquest period is rather like a jig-saw puzzle for which many of the pieces have been lost. Because of this we are only able to view but a small, tantalising portion of a much more comprehensive scene. In Yorkshire we are fortunate to have many of these pieces, although they may be faded and ill-fitting. Despite this, they provide an evocative image of English religion from that time, as well as an insight into the skill and artistic abilities of the Saxon stonemason.

Yorkshire's rich legacy of Saxon remains is exemplified in sites such as Kirk Hammerton (SE465555). Here the church has a nave and chancel surviving, some believe, from the 7th century, though a Saxon arch in the nave has at some time been damaged and subsequently repaired. All Saints parish church at Kirkby Hill (SE391683), just off the A1 near Boroughbridge, has some very fine Saxon reconstruction, and the sundial to be seen at St Gregory's (SE677858) in Kirkdale is exceptional, though an inscription dates this to the last years before the Norman Conquest.

Even further east, at Hackness near Scarborough, the chancel arch of St Peters (SE96909025) may date from the 8th century. Here, a monastery was established in the remote upper reaches of the Forge Valley. The carved stone cross contained in the aisle flanked by the Norman pillars may be an early 8th century monument to Oedilburgha, abbess of a monastery which was destroyed by Vikings in 867. The cross, though incomplete, has an inscription in runes, Latin and Old English.

Another St Peters, at Conisborough in South Yorkshire, is of Anglo-Saxon vintage. It has a nave that is Anglo-Saxon in form, being high and narrow with massive quoins. Furthermore, three small blocked-up windows above the Norman arches of the northern arcade, another above the south arcade and a fifth above the chancel arch are almost certainly from this period.

Other examples of early Saxon building can be examined at Skipwith church (SE657386) near Selby, where a 15th century belfry has been built upon the earlier tower, Little Ouseburn (SE452611) where stone from ruined Roman buildings was used to build the tower, and in York where the Anglian Tower (SE601523) was apparently built c. AD 600-700 to plug a gap in the Roman city walls. At Laughton-en-le-Morthen near Dinnington, the north door of All Saints'church (SK517882) is attributed to Anglo-Saxon masons, though the Normans saw fit to build a smaller door within it.

Among the finest and certainly the oldest Anglo-Saxon religious remains in the region are those preserved at Ledsham church (SE457298) near Leeds and in Ripon cathedral (SE314713) respectively. Ledsham is thought to be a foundation which started out as a royal monastic centre, and here we find stonework dating from about AD 700 in the almost complete nave, the base of the tower and an especially ornate south porch, though the carving here is attributed to a later period. Other notable features at Ledsham are the small blocked-up Anglo-Saxon windows in the south wall of the nave,

Plate 21: Ledsham church, the most complete Anglo-Saxon church in the region, may have originated as an important monastic centre. The tower, south porch and most of the nave are Anglo-Saxon in age.

either side of the present porch, and two carved fragments of a Saxon cross shaft set in the north wall opposite the entrance.

Some believe that Ledsham could be the building referred to by Bede in the year 731. According to Bede, a stone altar, said to have

Plate 22: The magnificently ornate Anglo-Saxon south porch at Ledsham.

come from an earlier wooden church, 'is kept to this day in the Minster of the Right Reverend priest and Abbot Thrydwulf standing in the forest of Elmet'. The completeness of the Anglo-Saxon church at Ledsham is all the more remarkable since it survived major renovation in the late 19th century.

Plate 23: This curiously-carved stone at Skipwith church, North Yorkshire, appears to depict a hunting scene.

The icing on the cake, however, has to be the 8th century crypt preserved beneath Ripon's magnificent cathedral. This is the only surviving fragment of a monastery founded by St Wilfred which was subsequently burned by the Danes in the 9th century, rebuilt and again destroyed by Eadred, first king of England, when he launched an attack on Northumbria in 948.

Many later churches were built upon foundations going back to Saxon times, the one at Tong (SE219306) near Bradford may be a case in question, though dating from the later Viking period. The village

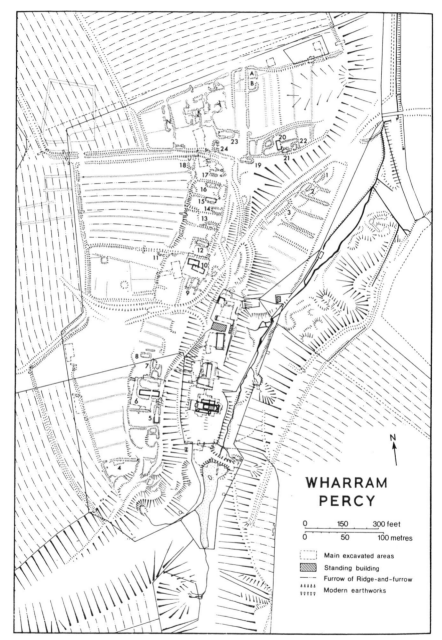

Fig. 18: Map of Wharram Percy, a deserted medieval village established on an important Scandinavian site. (Courtesy: Medieval Village Research Group.)

is mentioned in the Domesday Survey as Tving, being in the possession of a certain Steinulfr before it was handed over to the tenant Lord Ilbert. Churches in the Dales believed to post-date an Anglo-Saxon structure are St Wilfred's at Burnsall, also St Michael's in Hubberholme, St Oswald's at Arncliffe and Giggleswick's St Alkelda's.

In the East Riding, the deserted medieval village of Wharram Percy may have been the focus of a late 8th century minster church. Excavations within the nave of the present St Martins, the most complete building in the village, has revealed evidence for a small 10th century timber church beneath a later stone chapel on the same site. Elsewhere, in the south of the county, All Saints Parish church at Wath is partly Anglo-Saxon.

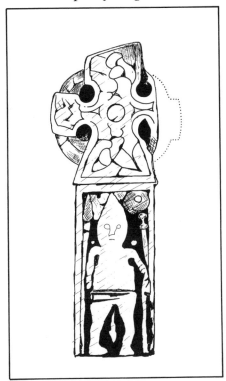

Fig. 19: Detail of Anglo-Scandinavian wheel-head cross located at Middleton on the southern limb of the North York Moors. The lower panel clearly depicts a warrior with sword, shield and spear.

Following the baptism of Edwin, the Roman Christian missionary Paulinus was installed in 625 as the first Bishop of York and subsequently travelled the northern countryside spreading the word as far as Swaledale where he wet the heads of many converts in the river by Catterick. Deira, and with it a large part of Yorkshire, became the religious front line in the Roman episcopal church struggle to win followers in the face of the rising tide of revitalized Celtic ritual form.

Sectarian gains on either side ebbed and flowed, and in Yorkshire this is reflected in the carved stone crosses which have survived (see Fig. 19). These display recurring themes representative of early Anglo-Saxon Christianity, while echoes of paganism in the bestial form are extant. Some crosses remain intact, others surviving only in fragmentary form, but in each we see religion mirrored as it was emerging in the late 6th to mid-7th centuries.

The difficulties in evaluating the purpose of these crosses lies in determining their original location, since more often than not they are discovered out of context at new locations. I think there is little doubt that many of these stoops marked consecrated ground where people gathered for worship before the erection of ecclesiastical buildings became vogue. The most complete specimens of Anglo-Saxon sculpted crosses can be seen at Masham (SE226807), at the church of St Peters (SE313330) in Leeds, inside which stands a thirteen-feet-tall partially reconstructed example, and at St Nicholas (SK267926) in High Bradfield west of Sheffield.

The circular cross shaft at Masham was one of the finest artifacts of the time but sadly, after many centuries, is in an advanced state of decay, undoubtedly accelerated by exposure to the corrosive atmosphere of the Industrial Revolution. It has carved panels in which rudely executed animals boldly parade the paganism of Yorkshire in the Dark Ages.

All Saints Parish Church at Ilkley (SE116478) houses three fine crosses dating from the 8th century, the tallest and best preserved being embellished with apostles and symbolic fighting beasts. Possibly the finest late English cross is the one inside Nunburnholme Church (SE848478), in the East Riding. This was discovered during restoration work between 1872 and 1873, when the south porch was removed, but since this may date from the Anglo-Danish years, I shall leave its description until later.

Doubtless there were many other crosses which have since disappeared at the hands of farmers seeking gateposts or received the destructive attention of iconoclasts such as King William of Normandy, the Scots or Oliver Cromwell's troops. Partially concealed in the grass verge beside the Stainforth to Halton Gill road at Rainscar, is the socket stone where another cross once stood. Whether the Ulfkill Cross (SD842714) dates from the Dark Ages is not clear. The name certainly sounds Germanic, resembling Ulfkettil, but it may have been a Middle Ages waymarker along the monastic road plied by the Cistercian monks from Fountains Abbey to their estates in the Lake District.

Some of the best incomplete crosses are to be seen at All Saints in Dewsbury, at Aldborough, Stonegrave near Malton, and at Bingley in the Aire Valley. In Wharfedale the churches at Collingham and Otley also house interesting fragments. Over on the east coast, the Whitby Abbey museum has on display an important collection of crosses which have surfaced over the years. These have survived in various states of completeness to symbolise religious life in the cliff top Anglian monastery founded here by Hilda in 657.

Crosses are still occasionally discovered, such as the one found in the river Wharfe near Burnsall by schoolchildren in 1984. What turned out upon examination to be the wheel head of a Viking period cross, was a few seconds away from being incarcerated into a wall the children were building as part of a conservation project in collaboration with the National Park.

Anglo-Saxon decoration has been found on artifacts other than crosses, including tombstones covers. There is a fine example at St Mary's (SD837581), in Long Preston on the A65 north-west of Skipton. Here, set in the floor at the north side of the chancel, the cover is inscribed with a cross and a pair of shears. East of Barnsley, All Saints church (SE418043) at Darfield also has a carved altar surround, possibly dating from the 8th century, which apparently came from an earlier foundation.

When land was being prepared for the building of the medieval monastery in Whitby, the foundation of the Anglo-Saxon church was revealed. All that remains of that great religious centre are a few artifacts such as glass beads, spindle whorls, fragments of amber, bowls, cooking pots and coins. Items of jewellery were unearthed and a comb inscribed with runes[16].

One of the county's more mysterious carved artifacts is located in the church at Skipwith near Selby. Set low down in the vestry wall, and concealed behind a small wooden door, this carving is obviously pre-Christian and seems to depict a group of men, one wearing some

---

16
    For an explanation of the runic alphabet, see Appendix 4

form of headgear, perhaps a helmet. It could represent a pig hunt since a boar-like beast seems to be biting the leg of one of the figures. In the outer wall of the tower is another stone described in the church literature as the 'bear stone', though one needs a vivid imagination to attach any features to it.

*   *   *

After seventeen years as the first Christian ruler of Northumbria, Edwin, and his son Osfrith, were fatally wounded on 12th October 632, in an engagement with Mercians in the southern marches of Deira. The battlefield is said by local tradition to have been at Slay Pits (SE677092), between Hatfield Woodhouse and the M18 motorway. This battle marked the beginning of a two-year offensive by Edwin's foster brother, Cadwallon and King Penda his Mercian ally, in which Northumbria was devastated. This victory destroyed much of the Roman ecclesiastical work of Paulinus thus allowing a late pagan Celtic revival to gain a precarious footing. Paulinus fled from York taking with him Edwin's widow and her children.

Northumbria then fell apart again into its constituent states of Deira and Bernicia. The latter reverted to its ancient royal household and, in a bid for the kingdom Eanfrith, the son of Æthelfrith was killed during a visit to Cadwallon to try to buy peace. Towards the close of 633, Cadwallon was defeated and killed and the state of Northumbria restored by Oswald, the brother of IEanfrith of Bernicia. By invitation from the new king, a company of monks came from St Colomba's Iona monastery. They settled on the rocky isle of Lindisfarne, and with Aidan established as its bishop, Christianity was restored.

The mixed fortunes of Northumbrian rulers in the closing years of the 7th century promised little hope of a long and prosperous reign, with few of the spoils normally resulting from victory on the battlefield. Instability was to remain the hallmark of the next 150 years during which Anglo-Saxon factions remained continually in a state of civil war. Northumbria suffered several vicious attacks from the south, directed at them by Penda, king of Wessex, aided no doubt by his heathen gods.

On 5th August, 641 Oswald fell in battle and was succeeded by Oswy, however the road to sovereign power was long and frequently provided a 'bumpy' journey. Oswy attempted to bribe Penda, but his hopes of buying peace from the Mercian leader fell upon deaf ears.

In the year 655 and with the prevailing weather to his advantage, Oswy's followers engaged an army led by the Wessex king. Penda was born a pagan and lived his entire life by the rule of the blade, forever seeking guidance from the deities. Subsequently he was to take his pagan beliefs with him to the grave, for surprisingly the day proved victorious for the hopelessly outnumbered Northumbrians. Penda was slain by a river which feeds the Humber, known to historians today only by the name Bede used, Winwaed.

Strife was not confined to secular affairs, but permeated every stratum of northern life, Christianity itself often being akin to a pool of calm in an ever-shifting sea of despair. In 659 Edwin's son, King Ethelwald, offered land for Cedd to set up a religious house from which to pursue the Celtic form of Christianity. There has been much discussion on the exact whereabouts of this foundation, somewhere on the southern limb of the North York Moors. Some believe the minster at St Gregory's (SE677858) in Kirkdale may have been where Cedd put down his divine roots. The 7th century church here was subsequently destroyed by Danes and later rebuilt by Orm, son of Gamel just before the Conquest.

Other scholars of Anglo-Saxon history prefer a second site, at Lastingham some four miles to the north-east, roughly midway between Kirkdale and Newtondale. From Bede we learn of an Anglo-Saxon monastery in Yorkshire, at a place called Laestinga eu (meaning island), which he describes as 'a site among some high and remote hills, which seemed more suitable for the dens of robbers'. The present Norman church (SE728905) at Lastingham is located in a secluded situation which might then have been described in such a manner. Within the crypt of the existing church are some carved stone fragments believed to have come from the original monastery. The very name Lastingham may refer to its situation, as an island of worship in a sea of paganism?

Two years earlier in 657, King Oswy founded a monastery at Streoneshalh[17] and appointed his daughter, the princess Hilda, as its first Abbess. This cliff-top religious centre, sometimes referred to as the Westminster of Northumbrian kings, flourished for a century after

Plate 24: The 11th century church of St. Gregory's, Kirkdale, was rebuilt by Orm, son of Gamel between 1055-65 and stands on an earlier foundation dating from the 7th century.

the death of Hilda in 680. The monastery was subsequently razed by the Danes, and replaced by the abbey we see today. It was ruined and abandoned following the dissolution of 1539, and reduced further by the shelling of German warships in 1914.

In more recent times, Whitby went on to achieve fame and fortune, not as a seat of religious abstinence, but as a centre for the jet carving industry, and as an important whaling port, captured so vividly in the evocative photography of Frank Meadow Sutcliffe. It was also where the famous captain James Cook served his apprenticeship, and later embarked upon his South Seas adventures. The whaling and jet industries have long since faded into insignificance, and it is many generations since anyone set out to plant the colonial flag on distant shores. However a local legend linked with Hilda lingers to this day, fostered to explain the profusion of fossil ammonites, or 'snakestones', found in the crumbling limestone cliffs hereabouts.

At the time of Hilda's arrival in Whitby, the area around the church was said to be overrun with venomous snakes. After first praying, she is reputed to have broken off the heads of all the serpents and cast them over the cliffs into the sea. As they fell, their writhing, headless bodies coiled up like clock springs and, upon striking the jagged rocks below, were instantly turned to stone. Ammonites do indeed resemble petrified snakes and one species in particular, *Hildoceras bifrons*, was named after the famous patron saint.

Five years after the founding of Whitby, a synod was convened there by King Oswy of Northumbria. Discussions apparently focussed on the positioning of Easter in the Christian calendar. St Wilfred argued the case for the Roman church while St Aiden, as Bishop of Lindisfarne, represented the regeneration of Celtic pagan beliefs. Rome won the day in yet another victory over the heathens, thus hammering home the final nail in the coffin of ancestral Celtic tradition in Yorkshire.

Although Christianity won the day at Whitby, English heathenism never really released its hold on the people. It is easy to see how the peasants tending their beasts and crops on their -*tuns* tucked away

---

17
The earliest name for Whitby

Plate 25: The Anglian tower, discovered at York in 1839, was built to fill a gap in the perimeter walls of Roman Eboracum in circa AD 650.

in remote corners of The Wolds and in the Pennine valleys would be little influenced by Whitby or whatever happened in York or elsewhere for that matter. They would no doubt continue to look to their pagan gods for guidance if it suited. That a deep-seated English heathenism never died is born out by the evidence.

Many elements of the English pagan calendar survive to this day. According to Bede, the start of the heathen year was December 25, corresponding to our Christmas Day. The last month of the old year and the first month of the new year were combined in the obscure Giuli, from which the modern name Yule and Yuletide are derived. Moreover, our season of Easter, which caused so much indecision at Whitby, embodies the name of the pagan goddess Eostre, the Old English name for the fourth month in the heathen year.

If the reader needs further proof that paganism lives on, our days of the week, Wednesday, Thursday and Friday, are dedicated to the pagan English gods and goddesses; for instance Woden, Thunor (Norse: Thor) the god of thunder and Frig (Norse: Frey). Though there is only circumstantial evidence for pre-Christian cult sites from this period, in the last chapter additional place-name evidence links these deities with features of the Yorkshire landscape.

The year after the synod of Whitby saw Wilfred established as bishop over a large area of Deira with his monastery at Ripon. All that has survives today of that religious centre are the remains of the crypt, which can still be seen in the undercroft of the present cathedral. Not many years afterwards Wilfred was to become Bishop of York.

In 670 Oswy succumbed to a fatal illness and, during the ensuing century, another nine Northumbrian kings lived out their strife-torn role. Like candles, each in turn burned briefly, flickered and was snuffed out – having cast some light, for good or evil, on the rich tapestry of Yorkshire in the Dark Ages. As king Ælfwald, the last of these dynastic rulers, was being murdered near Hadrian's Wall, an even worse calamity for the north was brooding off the coast of Northumbria.

6

A Thunderbolt from The North

They seek, are sought; to daily battle led,
shrink not, though far outnumbered by their foes
– Wm. Wordsworth

Motivated by wanderlust and the ill-gotten spoils of extortion, pillage
and piracy, the closing years of the 8th century witnessed the savage
Northmen plying the sea lanes around Britain's northern-most coastline. Viking raids around northern Britain had been taking place
sporadically for some time, but it was not until 793 that they were
accurately documented. In that year, a marauding band of Danes
landed at Lindisfarne and subjected the monastic centre and its
defenceless inmates to unrestrained attrition. Like a beacon, the seat
of religious focus for Northumbria burned furiously, radiating a grim
warning to the outlying lands of the north. Ripples of fear spread in
a kingdom soon to feel the crushing might of Thor's hammer. An entry
in the Anglo-Saxon Chronicle for that year vividly portrays the
impression that the first Danish incursion made on the population:

> In this year, terrible portents appeared over Northumbria, and miserably
> frightened the inhabitants: these were exceptional flashes of lightning,
> and fiery dragons were seen flying in the air. A great famine soon followed
> these signs; and, a little after that, in the same year on the Ides of January[18]
> the harrying of the heathen miserably destroyed God's church in
> Lindisfarne by rapine and slaughter.

In those superstitious times, natural phenomena such as a total

---

[18]
    More probably the Ides of June (8th June), a date provided by Simeon of
    Durham. It is hard also, to imagine the Vikings making a winter ocean crossing.

eclipse of the sun or the sudden appearance of a bright comet were often looked upon as evil omens and harbingers of doom. The Anglo-Saxon Chronicle makes many references to the 'hairy star'. The best documented instance was Halley's Comet, whose sudden appearance in 1066 foretold catastrophic defeat for the English at the Battle of Hastings. Whatever the nature of the portents that preceded the arrival of the Vikings at Lindisfarne, it was followed soon afterwards by the expected trouble and strife.

Halley's Comet re-appears once every 76 years and had appeared 31 years before the sacking of Lindisfarne. The fiery dragons seen in the sky were in all likelihood an impressive display of the northern lights (*Aurora Borealis*), though it could also have been a visit from a lesser comet, bearing in mind that a faint stellar object in those days would have been a far brighter object in the sky without the glare from today's cities.

With the English unable to marshal any effective resistance to such a sudden and quite unexpected onslaught, the Danes quickly gained the upper hand. Up and down the eastern seaboard, every inlet and estuary was to provide an open door for their shallow draughted vessels. Soon the invaders were boldly navigating their dragon-headed longships into the very heartland of Northumbria, here to vomit death and destruction upon the countryside and its people.

Soon, sad winds were sighing through the smouldering remains of hastily abandoned villages, and the charred shells of churches lay plundered and razed. The Viking bands, for armies they were not, advanced with confidence on foot, leaving nothing but a terrible waste at their heels, picked over by carrion quick to take advantage of a feast unlooked for. Slashed crops, burnt huts, everywhere the pathetic scars of wholesale destruction lay heavily on the land, above which rose a pall of smoke too, as from a funeral pyre.

They returned to their boats, driving slaves before them and bearing what loot they could shoulder, vanishing whence they had come, into the clammy grey mists of the northern sea. Heathen cries and the sound of ringing steel gradually faded away on the acrid breeze, leaving those who had survived traumatised, bloodied and dreading their return. And return they did, many times. The Anglo-Saxon dynastic kingdoms of 8th and 9th century England were reasonably prosperous despite the almost constant state of civil strife. No doubt it was this wealth and instability that made England easy prey for Viking pirates, drawn by the prospect of rich pickings that were unguarded and there for the taking.

Who or what were the Vikings and from what manner of nests did they issue forth, in the words of one contemporary scribe 'with a flotilla of ships, like stinging hornets'? The term Viking is derived from *Vikingar*, a name used to describe the northern races or *Noromenn* (Northmen) indigenous to the lands of the Baltic we know today as Denmark, Sweden and Norway. It may also be derived from *vik*, a Scandinavian name for bay, and 'Vikings' may be a term used for the people who plied these inlets with their craft.

Although each of these races shared common elements of genesis, language and culture, there is little evidence to suggest any great degree of nationalism. There were no rigid frontiers, and a warlike society engendered domestic insecurities there, as elsewhere in Europe during those troubled times.

The Viking Age is generally regarded among scholars of Scandinavian history, to be the period c.AD 780 to 1070, representing three hundred tumultuous years in which this northern people reached ascendancy as a seafaring race. It is during this period of history that the first landfall of Vikings in Britain is believed to have taken place c.780, in the far north, among the Orkneys and the Shetland Isles. Since they were essentially farmers, their aim here would not have been plunder and pillage, but a peaceful search for pastures new.

Almost a thousand years before the so-called Age of Migrations, the Viking movement had begun. It then subsided because of the convoluted power struggles between the neighbouring Scandinavian communities. The short, sharp sea-borne raids that became the hallmark of the Vikings in their heyday could not have taken place until their seaworthiness had come of age. This only came about with time, and was a gradual process born from the hard-earned skills gleaned from sailing the inshore waters – the viks and rugged fjords that indent the coastline of Scandinavia, and especially that of Norway.

Many factors are thought to have acted as catalyst for these migrations. Skills in oceanic navigation and the use of highly manoeuvrable craft were the means rather than the reason for the movement overseas. Historians see the widespread domestic use of iron, for ploughs and such like, coupled with rising population and an increasing demand for agricultural land as the major contributory factors. Norway for instance is an extremely mountainous country where farmland, confined to a narrow fertile strip sandwiched between the sea and the peaks, was at a premium.

Whatever the aspirations behind the trend it was to become the whole essence of life for the Scandinavian community, driven initially by the pressing urge for farmland, but later motivated by riches, fame and above all else, supreme power. These sentiments during the Viking Age were to sustain them during audacious journeys which took them southwards, across the Atlantic, east into continental Europe and Asia as far as Byzantium.

To be a Viking was elevated almost to that of a profession. Vikings ranged far and wide, establishing markets along a network of trade routes down which all manner of commodities were shipped: soapstone; gems; furs; salt; drink; metals and weapons. International trade had its unsavoury relative in piracy; the robbing and killing making the greatest impact upon those chronicling the first-hand encounters with the Vikings.

The pillage, wholesale destruction and land-taking that went with these raids, were second nature to colourful characters such as Eric Bloodaxe, Harald Bluetooth, Thorkell the Tall, Cnut and Sweyn Forkbeard. Whole communities were slaughtered in the pursuit of their business: a Viking warrior held little regard for life and property.

It is clear from the documentary evidence of those who survived that the initial encounters were traumatic for all concerned: the Vikings whose longships failed to safely negotiate the hazardous northern seas, and for those who suffered the brandishing of battle-axe or sword. It was irrelevant whether the hand wielding the fatal blade was Norse or Danish. Those upon whom the thunderbolt struck hardest referred to their attackers sometimes as Danes, and at other times as Norsemen. Even today it is difficult from the available evidence to distinguish between Norse Vikings and Danes; indeed it would appear that some raiding parties comprised both, even including warriors from Swedish Scandinavia.

However one views these first bloody encounters, they provided the prelude to a less violent conquest of Northumbria and Yorkshire. The Germanic origins of the Northmen and the English intermixed eventually in a more peaceful stirring of the north's cultural melting pot.

*   *   *

Following the destruction of Christian centres, we have to rely on the records of West Saxon scribes for scant details of the events that followed, and the later Domesday Survey for any indication of the extent of Danish influence. The study of place-names and their distribution is often given to support extensive settlement in Britain. However, in names with Danish or Anglo-Danish roots this does not necessarily indicate places where Scandinavians, Danes or otherwise, took to the plough.

Two place-name components *-by* and *-thorpe* are taken to be diagnostic of where settlers took a stance (Fig. 20). What must be understood however, is that the Vikings were rarely, if at all pioneers in the sense that they were carving out settlements and homesteads from virgin countryside; the landscape was already intensively farmed when they arrived. Their settlements were probably more by way of an infilling between the existing Anglo-Saxon *-tuns*.

At the time the Danes were arriving, land distribution and ownership were already undergoing radical changes. They may even have taken over Anglo-Saxon settlements before continuing identical agricultural practices. The suffix *-thorpe* is usually taken to indicate a satellite settlement, a farmstead or hamlet sited usually on lands belonging to a neighbouring or parent village, of Anglian roots. This fact is supported with names like Kirkby Malham, and in the Skipton area with parish names such as Burnsall-with-Thorpe, and Stirton-with-Thorlby, and in Thorpe Willoughby near Selby.

The *-by* name component is taken to be the equivalent of the Anglian *-tun* and represents settlements from a single homestead to a sizable hamlet. It was quite often combined with a personal name, for instance Thorlby and Thoralby, or else with a word indicating location or some obvious aspect of the landscape, for instance Kirkby Malham (the church near the settlement of Malham).

It was not until the latter half of the 9th century that raids on undefended monastic communities gave way to larger, more sustained attacks by armies bent upon invasion and widespread occupation. After more than three centuries of internecine warfare among the rival Northumbrian, Mercian and Wessex royal dynasties, England in the latter half of the 9th century was at last moving towards national unity. It was unfortunate timing that the Viking raven standard was again flying on English soil, heralding renewed troubles.

In the autumn of 865, Ubbi, with Halfdan and his brother Yngvarr (Ivar), alias the Boneless, both sons of the Viking 'freebooter' Ragnar Lodbrok, commanded a large-scale invasion fleet. Although its strength is not thought to have exceeded a thousand men, contemporary sources refer to these forces as the 'Great Army'. It seems to have been common practice of the scribes in the Anglo-Saxon Chronicle to exaggerate the size of these armies. Historians in later centuries tended to adopt this together with place-name evidence to support their argument for the widespread and complete settlement of Britain.

Place-names within the Danelaw which included personal name elements are largely absent from the landscapes of English England. It must be said though, that because a place has a Scandinavian element this is not definite proof that Danes were living there; a settlement would hardly be named by its inhabitants, as by their neighbours or those who had need for intercourse with its inhabitants, for instance for taxation purposes.

However extensive the Great Army was in reality, when it landed in c.865 it quickly established supremacy over the English. Over the next nine years, four of the established Anglo-Saxon royal kingdoms were conquered. With Northumbrian affairs forever in turmoil the Danes encountered little coherent resistance when in 866 Ivar the Boneless sailed his fleet up the Ouse and captured Eoforwik (York).

King Osberht had only recently been overthrown by Ella, and by the time these two opposing factions realised they were at risk from a common foe, the city had succumbed and both lay dead on the battlefield. Deira fell under Danish rule and soon afterwards Halfdan was declared the first overlord of the new Scandinavian principality of Jorvik. From then up until the time of the Norman conquest, York was to flourish as the most important town after London, the principal focus of Scandinavian power of either Dane or Norse origins. Halfdan installed Egbert as the puppet ruler of Jorvik and proceeded to divide up the rich farmlands of the old Northumbrian kingdom.

By 870, the territories of the East Angles had fallen and, two years later, an attempt to recapture York by the Northumbrians ousted Egbert. A large Danish army reasserted its martial authority the following year, appointing Ricsige as the new puppet king. Mercia collapsed three years later, and from that moment the previously coherent Danish forces divided. Halfdan returned north to Deira (Yorkshire east of the Pennines), which he was to use as a 'springboard' to wage repeated warfare on the Picts and Britons of Strathclyde, an action one assumes was justified to protect his northern frontier.

Meanwhile, the remaining Danish forces under Guthrum moved into East Anglia. These actions had repercussions for Deiran Yorkshire, since they were crucial to the invaders' designs on the first annexation of English soil. By the year 877, Yorkshire, along with the adjacent shires of Nottingham, Lincoln and Derby had ceased to be a part of English England.

In 878 Guthrum's army marched against Wessex, and early that year a mid-winter offensive caught the West Saxons completely by surprise. Alfred the Great, king of the West Saxons, suffered two crushing defeats and was later humiliated into buying peace on several occasions, the origin of the so-called Danegeld.[19] The defeat of the West Saxons sounded the death knell for the English kingdoms further north. For almost a century it was to be the Viking sword as much as the plough that would shape future events of the land. York remained under Danish influence until 919 when the Norse invaders drove them out.

By late 885, much of Anglo-Saxon England was ruled under the jurisdiction of the so-called Danelaw. By definition, this was that part of England no longer under English influence, but subject to Danish laws, customs and language. It included all of Northumbria. Its

---

19
  Best described as protection money.

southern boundary, as determined by a treaty between King Alfred of Wessex and Guthrum in about 886, was marked by the line of the River Thames upstream to London; then more or less corresponded to the north-westerly course of Watling Street, the Roman road linking London with Chester (see Fig. 20).

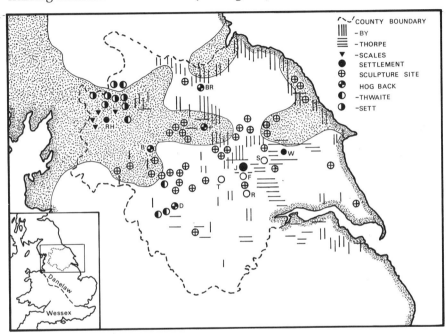

Fig. 20: Viking Age Yorkshire showing principal historic sites and distribution of Scandinavian place-name components. Inset shows the southern limit of the influence of the Danelaw: BR) Brompton; RH) Ribblehead; P) Pickhill; B) Burnsall; W) Wharram Percy; S) Stamford Bridge; J) Jorvik; F) Fulford; T) Tadcaster; R) Riccal; D) Dewsbury.

Within the bounds of the Danelaw, the -*thorpe* place-name component is concentrated into a wide corridor curving from the Midlands through Lincolnshire and sweeping back across the Yorkshire Wolds and up the Vale of York toward Ripon. The Domesday Survey gives over 200 instances of -*by* within Yorkshire, mostly concentrated in the Vale of York. Over 90 percent of these are combined with personal names of Scandinavian origin, a fact not justified by settlement of the invading armies alone.

The Domesday book records 155 place-names for Yorkshire ending in the suffix *-thorpe*. Outside this belt however, the incidence of *-thorpe* and *-by* thins out, though others certainly existed. The Medieval Village Research Group lists for the East Riding the sites of thirty-five 'lost' villages with the *-thorpe* suffix, eight for the West Riding and in the North Riding nineteen *-thorpe* villages, all of which have long ago disappeared. Moreover some fifty-six settlements in *-by* have also vanished throughout the county.

The problem of land erosion along Yorkshire's Holderness coastline was highlighted in the third chapter. Further proof of the devastating effect of the North Sea is to be found in the Domesday Survey. Here the roll-call of villages lost beneath the waves number twenty-nine along the thirty-nine miles of coast between Flamborough Head and Spurn Point. Thorpe villages lost in this manner include Pockthorpe (TA039634), Swaythorpe (TA038691), Easthorpe (SE877455), Low Caythorpe (TA117677), Towthorpe (SE867438), Wilsthorpe (TA173656) and Ravensthorpe (TA005426). Others would have been devastated in the scorched earth policy implemented by William of Normandy, while others never recovered from the great plagues of the 14th century.

Tuke's map of 1786 marks the location of the church of Old Aldbrough some way off the coast and some distance from the present village. An inscribed stone, believed to be Anglo-Danish and to have come from the lost church, is now housed in the present village church. According to other sources, two other Danish settlements, suffered the same briny fate. The once thriving village of Tharlesthorpe was located in the Humber on Sunk Island at the time when this was separated from the mainland by a small channel. Sunthorpe too, was positioned due south of Easington at about the same latitude as present-day Kilnsea.

The dramatic way in which the coastline and the mouth of the Humber have shifted over the centuries means that the sites of many places for which there are records are now some way seaward (see Fig. 15). Also on Tuke's map can be found Ravenser and Ravenser Odd, two villages whose ghosts are buried somewhere in the shifting sands of the estuary to the west of the spit of land leading to Spurn Head. Ravenser seems to have held some importance for the Danes in the early 11th century, since it is mentioned twice in Icelandic texts relating to the battle of Stamford Bridge.

Long after that momentous date, Ravenser developed into an important coastal centre. In 1305 it returned two members of Parliament and five years later sent warships to join the expeditionary force of Edward II to Scotland. Moreover, the siege of Calais benefited from a ship registered at Ravenser. Even as far back as 1346 the village was suffering the insidious encroachments of the sea and in 1471 Edward IV reported upon his visit, that the port was being seriously undermined by the sea. The king's antiquary John Leland appears to have been the last dignitary to visit Ravenser, after which it disappears completely from the records.

*   *   *

Yorkshire of course fell wholly within the bounds of the Danelaw. For the purpose of administration the county was divided by the Danes into *thridings*, from which have subsequently emerged the old East, West and North Ridings, county divisions that have endured over a thousand years until the boundary changes of 1974.

These *thridings* had their roots grounded in the old Norse *riojungr*, meaning a third part. They were further subdivided into *wapentakes*, a smaller unit derived from the Old Norse *vapnatak*. A wapentake represented the symbolic brandishing of arms, or 'weapon taking' by which assent was given for decisions taken by a leader. Its Anglo-Saxon equivalent was the Hundred, an administrative unit comprising one hundred hides. This was a notional land measure, varying from time to time, but generally being the amount of land that an eight-ox plough team could usually maintain under cultivation, in modern terms nominally about 120 acres.

Weapon taking usually took place at a 'thing' or moot place, an important gathering point for meetings and decision making. This may have been held on a prominent hill or mound, perhaps by an ancient tree. The withered stump of one venerable oak, which may have been the site of a moot, was until the early part of this century still hanging onto life beside the A660 at Headingley in Leeds. Two public houses nearby were named in memory of the great tree. One of them, the Skyrack takes its name from the Old English *scir* (shire) and *ak* (oak) of the Saxons, who themselves were not unfamiliar with the custom of meeting beneath sacred trees.

It has been suggested (Raistrick), that moot place or moot hill survives today in the modern mutlow, mucklow and micklow. A similar-sounding name is found in *mickle*, a component found, for example, in Mickle Fell and in the Airedale village Micklethwaite. *Thwaite* is also a Scandinavian element given to represent the place where a settlement was located in a forest clearing, often inclined towards a marsh, lake or river. Perhaps Micklethwaite evolved as a place where important meetings had originally been convened in a woodland glade? The village of Kirkby Malham has Anglo-Danish roots and only a half mile to the north-west we find Micklaw Hill (SD887615), perhaps the moot place for the Vikings of Malhamdale?

Whatever we think of the Vikings today, no matter how repugnant their murderous behaviour, or their outright contempt for life and property, the Northmen, like the Anglo-Saxon predecessors, left behind important elements of their native tongue to append and enlarge the hybrid Germanic language we call English. The Danes prevailed so intensely upon the English that the reader might be surprised just how much of the *Donsk Tunga* still lingers in everyday use. Apart from place-names already discussed, words such as drown, happy, law, by-law, leg, reef, ugly, rift, egg, birth, skull and scare represent just a few commonplace examples. Many sayings and turns of speech may be attributable to these early influences. Perhaps 'sackless', a northern vulgar term for someone who is a bit on the simple side, also originates from the Old Norse *sacleas*, meaning innocent?

The landscape also bears witness to their lasting influence. In Danish mythology the raven is a bird endowed with strange powers, hence its use as a motif for the Danish standard. They appeared in several Scandinavian sagas and from these sources were symbolic of valour and overriding victory in warfare. In some poems the birds seem to have actually taken part in battles, notably in one work by the Icelandic poet Egill Skallagrimsson, in which Erik Bloodaxe of Norway is extolled as a warrior in hostilities both at home and in foreign parts.

The traditional link with these mysterious cult birds may account for the naming of Ravenser, the lost Humber port. Is it possible that other places may have received the attention of Viking settlers who, out of reverence for these birds, named many prominent features of the landscape? There is a group of rocks known as the Raven Stones

(SE119580) on Rocking Moor, east of Barden Fell, and a Raven Peak (SE139553) some two miles to the south-east of there. Other possible links with the Yorkshire landscape include Raven Stones Moor (SE105648) near Greenhow, Raven's Gill (SE152638) near Pately Bridge, and in the Yorkshire Dales National Park at Raven Ray (SD696754). In the east of the region there is Ravenscar (NZ298013) and the once-important Humber port of Ravenser.

In the years between the treaty of 886 to King Alfred's death in 899 Mercia, Wessex and Northumbria had almost continually been embroiled in one war after another, with the Danes already settled within the Danelaw and new Danish forces raiding from across the channel. During this time Jorvik (York) remained under Danish influence, governed by a succession of Viking monarchs. Wessex had proved a difficult nut to crack since Alfred had learnt the lessons of earlier defeats and was better prepared than when Guthrum's forces first caught the West Saxons napping.

*　　*　　*

As the tenth century opened, a new wave of invaders arrived in Yorkshire, this time migrating from north-west Norway via the Orkneys and Shetlands, to the north-west isles of Scotland and ultimately into Ireland. From here these Norsemen penetrated mainland Britain via the Isle of Man and the north-west coast. By the middle of the 10th century their sphere of influence was extended up the west side of the Pennines.

They were probably second or third generation settlers, since they brought with them strong Celtic undertones mingled with their own culture. There was little friction between the new invaders and the Anglo-Danish people already settled in the lowland valleys. Penetrating eastwards, the Norse moved into the Yorkshire Dales where they had a preference for the upland fells and steep valley heads, where sheep runs were established above the tree-line.

In the main these marginal lands had long been neglected by Anglo-Danish interests, the Norse farmers finding only a thin veneer of lingering Celtic tradition still in existence. Norse influence is most noticeable in the Yorkshire Dales in the Craven region, in areas of the Pennines in the south of the county and within isolated pockets scattered throughout the North York Moors, to which they migrated from the Lake District via Stainmore. Their settlements take the form of isolated farmsteads rather than nucleated villages.

To a hill farmer ranging over a wide expanse of fell country, topographical features would have been as important as are street names and architectural landmarks to a modern city dweller. The wild landscapes of The Dales, the Pennines and North York Moors reminded the Norse settlers of their homeland, so they tended to confine themselves to the upper reaches of the valleys. Here we find concentrations of Norse terminology for features of the landscape. Gill, beck, clint, heath, fell, moss, mere, keld (a spring), foss (waterfall), raike (steeply rising ground), cam, tarn, ling, berg (a rock), grain (a branch or fork in a river or stream) and bield (a sheltered place) are a few examples still in common use throughout the Dales region.

We find these components embodied in such place-names as Castleberg, Fossgill, Meregill, Black Keld, Ling Gill, Buckden Rake and Cam Houses. Several instances of the Norse *vincle*, meaning an angle or corner, survive in the many Finkle Streets, winding thoroughfares to be found in towns like York, Knaresborough, Richmond and Malham. Still in Malhamdale, the name Trenhouse probably derives from *trani*, meaning wild birch, and frequent instances of -*mark* on Malham moor signify common pasture.

The Norse place-name suffix -*thwaite* (a forest clearing) is not nearly so common in Yorkshire as the Danish -*Thorpe*. However, we have many examples, most of which we find in what would have been remote country. *Thwaite* village in the upper reaches of Swaledale, Langthwaite, Slaithwaite, Linthwaite, and Micklethwaite in the Aire Valley. The name also occurs in a few places along the southern edge of the North York Moors but is absent from the predominantly Danish Wolds region. The Irish-Norse influence is apparent in Langstrothdale at Yockenthwaite, a name derived from the obvious combination of the Norse element with the Irish-Norse personal name Eogan.

Except for the Lake District, in Cumbria, where settlement was almost complete, nowhere is Norse influence more noticeable than in the Yorkshire Dales. Areas such as upper Chapel-le-Dale and Ribblehead evoke the landscape settled by these Norse pioneers, and though many local farmsteads are probably sited on foundations established in the last two centuries before the Norman Conquest, few remains have survived.

The one exception is that found at Gauber High Pasture on the northern flank of Park Fell. On this late 9th century site (SD766784) are the foundations of a Nordic farmstead incorporated into a nearby three-acre field system. The settlement includes a long house of almost 70 feet in length (see Fig. 21), as well as a nearby smithy and bakery, all three buildings having apparently been linked by stone pathways. The foundations of the buildings, which had turfed roofs, show that the walls were some five feet thick. This site is not obvious until right next to it, then is seen clearly on the edge of limestone pavements (clints) some 220 yards due south of Gauber Quarry.

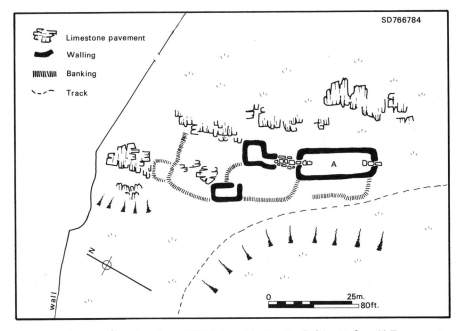

Fig. 21: Viking settlement site at Ribblehead in the Yorkshire Dales: A) Represents the foundations of a longhouse.

All around the Ribblehead site, we find place-names with recognisable Norse terminations: -*scale* (from the old Norse *skali* for an isolated farmstead) occurs today in Low Scales, Southerscales and

Winterscales, while the more common -*rigg* element is found along the east and southern slopes of Simon Fell and Ingleborough Hill respectively, and again in the vicinity of the drumlins[20] between Ling Gill and Gearstones. In the North York Moors region -*rigg* occurs quite frequently especially applied to long ridge lines.

Where the Norse farmers had their spring shielings we find another common name in -*sett*, derived from the Norse *saetre*. This is reflected in the names of one group of hamlets near Hawes, in Wensleydale, at Appersett, Burtasett, Countersett and Marsett, while in nearby Cotterdale there is an area called Humesett. Elsewhere, in Sleddale is Swinesett Hill, on Great Shunner Fell a moorland region named Pickersett, and not to be left out, Garsdale has its Holmesett Hill.

Plate 26: Countersett village, in the Yorkshire Dales, is one of several in the area founded upon the site of a Norse farmstead, a saetr, from which the village derives its name.

20
   Rounded hills of glacial drift.

Others examples exist on the flanks of Whernside, Langsett village near Penistone, in the south of the county, and at Wintersett village near Wakefield. The Scandinavian name is also present in the variants *-seat* and *-side*, as in Selside in Upper Ribblesdale and Great Pinseat north of Swaledale. In Swaledale, Gunnerside provides another instance where the name for a feature of the landscape has been combined with a personal name, in this case Gunnerside being 'the spring shieling of Gunnar'.

More substantial evidence of Nordic influence is manifested in religious artifacts, particularly in carved icons. The 10th and 11th centuries brought ideas which influenced their style, the wheel-head cross in particular being a Celtic concept. The so-called hog-back tomb is usually associated with the Vikings. Fragments can be seen in the Richmondshire Museum, and complete examples have also survived.

The most remarkable group of hogbacks is to be found in the church at Brompton-on-Swale near Northallerton. The three specimens here display carved covers which appear to reflect the pitched roof of a long-house. Each end is clasped by a bear. Others specimens are preserved in Burnsall church, at Dewsbury and Pickhill near Thirsk. Also in the church at Brompton is the interesting Cockshaft Cross depicting an 8th century scene in which bestial images are locked in combat.

The superb cross to be seen in St James church at Nunburnholme may be an artifact belonging to the 8th or 9th centuries, if the content of its carved panels is any measure. The upper section of the shaft was found embedded in the east wall of the old porch, the lower segment having been discovered close to the south wall of the Nave. It is thought that the missing head and middle section could still be buried in the wall or foundations of the Nave.

Other crosses, or fragments of them include the late 9th century Anglo-Scandinavian cross in Hackness church near Scarborough. Carved wheel head crosses may also be seen at Middleton church near Pickering, North Frodingham, near Great Driffield, and around the lower reaches of the Swale, at Gilling, and Finghall. York has several surviving examples of Viking sculpture, principally at the Minster, the former priory of the Holy Trinity, in the churches of St

Mary and St Denys, and within All Saints church at the junction of Ousegate with Coppergate.

Although King Alfred's reign had been blighted by repeated troubles with the capricious Danes, it is to his credit that England avoided being annexed as a whole. Upon Alfred's death Edward the Elder acceded to the throne of Wessex and the vision of a united country took one more step nearer to reality. Following the centuries-long struggle by the English to establish Germanic kingdoms in England, King Edward succeeded, before his death in the year 924, in winning back all of the territory under the Danelaw south of the Humber.

Despite the English gains, York in the 9th and 10th centuries was a thriving Viking commercial centre and was ruled by a succession of both Norwegian and Danish overlords. The town enjoyed trade from all around mainland Europe, north Africa and Asia Minor. Items of Scandinavian jewellery have appeared in the East Riding, while Whitby jet has turned up in Scandinavian burial sites. The excavations at the York Coppergate site between 1976 and 1981 revealed a flourishing industry in textiles, metalwork, leather craft, woodware and glass blowing. Other objects unearthed offer further proof of the widespread trade centred upon the Norse-Irish kingdom and included shells from as far away as the Red Sea.

As the dig progressed, archaeologists uncovered complete houses and workshops, many still containing everyday utensils, tools and clothing. The magnificence of Viking Age Jorvik, revealed from the richness of the Coppergate excavations, is incorporated into the Jorvik Centre and Museum. In 'time cars' the visitor is whisked back in time to York as it was a thousand years ago, to see, smell and hear life in 9th century, complete with reconstructed streets with dwellings, a market and wharf. The archaeological dig itself has also been reproduced and together with the countless artifacts that were unearthed, the Jorvik Centre represents the finest insight into Viking Age Yorkshire.

Many of York's street names retain their Scandinavian origins. The suffix -*gate* is derived from the Norse *gata*, meaning street, but one must not be fooled into believing translation is quite so simple. Place-name analysis is fraught with pit falls. Swinegate would quite definitely be the street of the pigs but what of Coppergate and

Goodramgate. The former has no connection with that familiar base metal, but was the street of the cup makers. Again Goodramgate has nothing at all to do with well-behaved ruminants, being the street of Guthram. Elsewhere in the county there is hardly a town or city that does not have -*gate* place-names, most commonly Kirkgate, the thoroughfare leading to the church.

*   *   *

When the Vikings settled in England, they were ardent pagans. They brought with them not only their skill in farming, metal smelting and a demonstrable expertise in mobile warfare, but also their traditions and a rich mythology inhabited by many fanciful beasts and powerful gods. During the Viking age the gods most celebrated among the northern cultures were Odinn, Frey and Thor.

In Scandinavian mythology the gods created Midgard, the world of mortal men, at the centre of which was Asgard, the residences of those deities. In Asgard stood Valholl, the hall of the slain, to which went the most valiant of warriors who fell in battle. The hall was presided over by Odinn who was demonic, capricious and frightening, the foremost of northern gods. Thor too, was a force to be respected. In some regions of the motherland he was the god of agriculture, but away in foreign lands it was Thor's hammer, not the sickle, that most strongly opposed Christianity.

Central to this created world of the northern gods was the tree of life, the *yggdrasill*, whose extending limbs reached the sky and embraced the earth. It had three roots reaching out to the realm of the dead, the home of the frost giants and to the world of mortal men. More significantly, beneath the tree of life, where it stood in Asgard, was the most venerated seat of the gods; under the roots was the Well of Wisdom and Fate, where dwelt the three Norns, Urd (fate), Skuld (necessity or future) and Verdandi (present). The Norns each day refreshed the tree of life from the well beneath its feet and on this depended the future well-being of the world.

In Yorkshire we find three important connections with this pagan mythology. One of the famed Viking crosses located in Ilkley's All Saints church is adorned with a relief carving believed by some to represent the Norse tree of life. Moreover, at the prominent hill of

Roseberry Topping (NZ578126), near Great Ayton, in the East Riding, there is a more significant link with pagan worship. An early name for this striking, conical-shaped hill is Othensberg. Berg comes from the Norse for rock or mountain, while the prefix 'othens' is thought to be a corruption of Odinn.

Also in the same neighbourhood we come across two place-names given to standing stones, that lend further weight to theories that Viking paganism gained more than a toe-hold in the North York Moors region. The stones are called Nanna and Old Wife. Nanna and Nanny are names known in the past to have been linked with witchcraft in this country, however the Nanna of Norse mythology was the goddess of nature and wife of Balder, who was the son of Odinn. On Fylingdales Moor (NZ905022) Old Wife's Neck is the name given to a standing stone, in Norse mythology Old Wife is said to represent the Viking earth Mother.

Odinn was not the only Norse god to have been dedicated in features around the Yorkshire countryside. Freeborough Hill (NZ690127) may be named after Frey, the Goddess of fertility, while Thor, the god of thunder, is enshrined in ancient wells, many of which were later canonised by missionaries who saw fit to dedicate them to Christian Saints.

In the Yorkshire Dales there is Thoragill (SD890702), and east of there, in upper Wharfedale, two wells clearly retaining their pagan associations. About a hundred yards below Hebden in the beck which divides the village, we find Thruskell Well (SE028628), now unfortunately incorporated into the water supply for a trout farm. Further south, near Burnsall (SE027608) is the Thorskell Well. Whether any of these sites represented the Well of Wisdom and Fate for the Scandinavian settlers we will never know.

Guy Ragland Phillips[21] draws a parallel between the Norse *yggdrasill* and the Tree of Life Stone on Snowden Carr. However, take a stroll across the moors to this composite cup and ring carving and you will not find the world ash tree of Scandinavian folklore, merely an isolated holly bush rattling in the breeze. Like the rock carvings

---

21
Brigantia

concentrated on Rombald's Moor, across the valley, the Tree of Life Stone is also dated to the late Neolithic or early Bronze Age.

Adjacent to the Great North Road by Boroughbridge are the three famous Devil's Arrows, referred to in Chapter Two. Less famous but infinitely more mysterious is the Devil Stone seen in the village of Copgrove (SE345635) six miles south from Ripon. At the eastern approach to the village is the parish church of St Michael and All Angels. The Devil Stone was incorporated into the outside of the north-east wall when major alterations took place in the last century. Although badly weathered, the carved Stone does appear to portray a figure, possibly wearing a helmet, and may be holding some tool or

Plate 27: The curious Devil Stone, built into the wall of St. Michael's church, Copgrove. Is it a representation of the Norse god Thor and his hammer?

weapon in its right hand. To the left of the figure an emblem resembles the letter 'T' or possibly a hammer.

The Craven District of The Dales has given rise to the legend of St Dunstan and which is related briefly in the following rhyme. In these lines and the explanation offered by Dixon[22], we may draw too many parallels for these to be mere coincidence.

> St Dunstan, as the story goes,
> Seized the Devil by his nose
> With red-hot tongs, and made him roar:
> They heard him twenty miles and more.

In Norse mythology, clear views were held concerning how the world began and in what form doom awaited, concepts which are preserved in the prose work, Edda, written by Snorri Sturluson (c.1220). Accordingly we learn of the punishment of Loki in Asgard, the home of the gods, for his part in the treachery resulting in the death of Odinn's son, Balder the Beautiful at Ragnarok, the world's end.

The St Dunstan story may be a distorted rendering of Norse folk-tradition relating to the punishment of Loki. In this context Loki the evil one, is represented by the Devil and Thor by St Dunstan. The latter is obviously a smith for he seizes the Devil with red-hot tongs. In his earthly form, Thor also was a smith amongst other things. We learn that Thor is in his workshop when a suspicious character wanders in, none other than Loki. The latter tempts Thor with promises of power, wealth and a life of idleness, but at the cost of becoming subservient to Loki and forever after to dwell in Hel, the antecedent of Valholl.

Norse mythology, as told in the Edda, tells how Balder was killed by a sprig of mistletoe hurled at him by his brother Hod at the instigation of the evil Loki. In the St Dunstan legend Loki's crime is the temptation of Thor with lethargy, riches and potency, and for which retribution comes swift. When Thor succeeds in luring the evil one into a large sack supposedly filled with provisions for the long journey to Hel, he draws it fast, and placing the sack on his anvil, proceeds to beat Loki with his largest hammer until he roars to be

---

22
   Chronicles and Stories of the Craven Dales, 1881.

released on penance of immediate departure, never to tempt the blacksmith ever again.

Loki is despatched to Asgard where Thor and the other gods dwell. He is then imprisoned surrounded by venomous serpents. Thor was the Scandinavian god of thunder and warfare. He took his place in the overall picture of pagan polytheism by opposing Christianity, commanding the heavens and wielding a thunderbolt for a hammer. In the world of mortal men however, he was a blacksmith with just such a hammer as may be portrayed on the Copgrove stone.

Whether this mysterious artifact relates to the St Dunstan legend, to Thor and his hammer, or indeed any pagan deity I shall leave the reader to contemplate. Whatever its origins or the aspirations of the mason who carved the stone, it is clearly of some antiquity and would appear to be pre-Christian. The church itself is ancient, being mentioned in the Domesday Book, and may have been erected on the site of a pagan shrine. The proximity of eSt Mungo's Well seems to lend substance to such a theory.

The Devil Stone is pagan in appearance, judging by its accentuated sexual organs and the hammer-like motif, indicative of one of the oldest artifacts in the country. It may be the only surviving artifact salvaged from such a heathen site of worship. A carving, found on the shaft of a 10th century wheel-head cross in the Holy Trinity church at Stonegrave, near Malton, bears some similarities to the features on the Copgrove stone.

For almost a century since Halfdan divided the old Anglo-Saxon estates, York was to remain the focus of Viking England. The last of the Scandinavian kings to rule from here was Erik Bloodaxe, who in 947 invested Norse power for a time in a shaky alliance between York and Dublin. Erik was the son of Harald Fairhair, king of Norway, whom he later succeeded. After a short but tumultuous reign, he was twice ousted from York, each time retreating to the north. And it was here around 954 that he finally fell by the sword of his enemies at the battle of Stainmore, a bleak land forming the frontier between York-shire and Durham.

From the beginning of the 11th century, events were taking shape that would lead eventually to the most important change in English history since the Roman invasion. In the year 1018 Godwin, Earl of

Wessex, was probably the most powerful figure in the country after the king, Edward the Confessor. The following year Godwin took Gytha as his bride, a union which produced six sons and three daughters. Two of his sons, Tostig and his elder brother Harold, received their earldoms in 1055 and 1044 respectively. They were both eventually to play important roles in English destiny, as it happened on opposing sides.

As Earl of Northumbria Tostig introduced unwelcome taxes and in 1065 had two nobles murdered. One of these unfortunates we know was Orm, son of Gamal, and at the southern fringe of the North York Moors an artifact is linked with this treachery. The carved sundial at St Gregory's Minster church in Kirkdale (SE677858) is one of the finest late Saxon artifacts in the region and includes an inscription, in Northumbrian English, which relates how one Orm, son of Gamal,

Plate 28: The Anglo-Saxon sundial built into St. Gregory's parish church, Kirkdale, is one of the best preserved in the country. The 11th-century inscription, in Northumbrian English, relates that: 'Orm, Gamel's son bought St Gregory's Minster when it was all broken down and fallen, and he let it be made anew from the ground to Christ and to St Gregory in the days of Edward the King and Tosti the Earl. And Haward wrought and Brand Priests'.

acquired the church in a ruinous state and had it rebuilt in the days of Edward the King and Tosti the Earl.

Tostig had failed miserably in his duties as Earl of Northumbria and was subsequently ostracised for his crimes against the people. In the end rebellion surfaced in the autumn of 1065, at which Tostig went into hiding across the channel. He orchestrated a military come-back which in the event was defeated, and he only put in another appearance, his final one as it happened, when in 1066 he joined forces with a Norwegian battle fleet that had appeared in English waters.

Harald Hardradi was a Viking in every sense of the word, descended from Harald Fairhair, the father of Erik Bloodaxe. In 1047 he became King of Norway, a reign mostly taken up with a long-running conflict with his rival Sweyn Forkbeard of Denmark. Harald the 'ruthless' had amassed a small fortune in booty as a result of his conquests and campaigns in eastern Europe, Asia Minor and in Mesopotamia. He was a powerful man who sought to increase his sphere of influence. In 1064 a final peace was made with Denmark, after which Harald turned his attention to the conquest of England.

When the childless Edward the Confessor died in January 1066 he bequeathed the throne of England to Harold Godwinsson and unwittingly hammered home the final nail in the coffin of the recently united Anglo-Saxon England. William of Normandy was incensed when Harold was crowned king of England and had, through his aunt, the Norman mother of Edward the Confessor, proclaimed himself the rightful heir to the English throne. Moreover, at whatever cost, he would install himself as the new monarch.

*   *   *

We now move to the final swing of the pendulum, towards the end of summer, 1066. Harold knew that he would have to fight to remain king. His main adversaries were recognised as Duke William of Normandy, his own brother Tostig and Norway's Harald Hardradi. It was unfortunate for Harold that all three of his enemies should decide simultaneously to embark upon conquest.

In the autumn of 1066, the large invasion fleet which Hardradi had been assembling in Scandinavian coastal waters sailed for Britain.

Expecting attack from across the channel, Harold, earl of Wessex, had been guarding the southern coastline when he received word of the Viking fleet. In the autumn the large Norwegian armada had crossed the North Sea and was moving south down the coast of Northumbria, wreaking mayhem on everything in its path. Harold set out immediately northwards to counter this threat, safe in the knowledge that the weather conditions prevailing in the channel would prevent William's ships from sailing. Unfortunately those same winds which proved the bane of William allowed Hardradi's fleet to make good speed.

Along the way Tostig's ships joined forces with the Norwegians and together they sailed undetected into the mouth of the Humber. They slowly proceeded upstream, still in secrecy, as far as Riccal (SE609382) where the combined forces disembarked. From here Harald and Tostig marched their army north to Gate Fulford (SE610612), a little south of York, where they met and defeated Edwin, Earl of Mercia, and Morcar, Earl of Northumbria, on Tuesday 20th September. Marching on into York the Vikings met with little if any resistance, took tribute and provisions, and returned to their ships.

By this time, Harold was proceeding north with great haste (see Fig. 22). The surviving Roman military roads were still in good shape, and by putting these to good use he made remarkable time. Following Ermine Street to Lincoln, he passed on through Doncaster to Castleford, where his troops crossed the river Aire, probably the most hazardous point on the march. Continuing north-east they reached Tadcaster (SE487435) and on the 24th a rendezvous with the remnants of the small English fleet anchored on the Wharfe.

Having been promised further hostages Hardradi had disembarked his ships again and marched upon Stamford Bridge (SE715555) on the river Derwent, presumably to receive this tribute as was the Viking custom. The Norwegians were situated on the east side of the river, where on the 25th September they were surprised by King Harold's forces and overwhelmingly crushed.

According to the Anglo-Saxon Chronicle, the two armies fought a day-long battle, during which both the Norwegian leader and Harold's own traitor brother were killed. Of the three hundred ships bringing the invaders, only twenty-four were needed to carry the survivors back to their homeland. The scale of the Norwegian defeat is indicated by the fact that, on average, a Viking longboat carried thirty men. The Battle of Stamford Bridge proved a decisive victory for the English but, ironically, was to help the Bastard of Normandy in his invasion. Harold's army was battle-weary and over 200 miles from the impending threat on the country's south coast.

Two days after the battle at Stamford Bridge the weather in the channel changed and Duke William ordered his fleet to sea. They landed on the south coast of England on the 28th September. By the 1st October news of this development had somehow reached Harold and for the second time in as many weeks he urgently led his forces to battle, arriving at London after an amazing forced march of only four days.

Here he remained for a week while his men rested, providing the opportunity to marshal further reinforcements before setting out for Sussex. On the 14th October, Harold's forces and William's army joined battle at Hastings with an outcome that is well-documented. It signalled the end of Anglo-Saxon England.

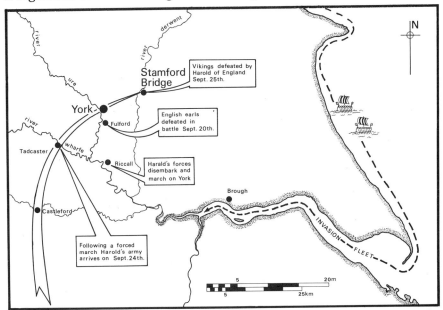

Fig. 22: Map of east Yorkshire showing the events leading up to the decisive Battle of Stamford Bridge.

Appendix One

Major Prehistoric Sites

Only those sites are included where there are substantial remains
worth seeing.

NZ 461103   Castle Hill, ½ mile N.W. of Middleton-on-Leven.
             Earthwork, perhaps a hill fort, in a commanding
             position overlooking the River Leven.

NZ 708640   A solitary standing stone, may be a remnant of a
             Bronze Age circle.

NZ 856037   Sleights Moor. An area of Neolithic barrows.

NZ 905022   Old Wife's Neck. Two standing stones on Fylingdales
             Moor, amid system of earthwork trenches.

SD180504   Tree of Life Stone. Located on Snowden Carr,
             overlooking Washburn Valley. Another cup and ring
             composite.

SD785666   Sewell's Cave. Important Romano-British remains
             unearthed in seat earths.

SD839650   Victoria Cave, near Settle. Mesolithic occupation site.

SD842642   Attermire Cave, near Settle. Neolithic occupation site.
             Also revealed artifact of Romano-British age.

SD876894   Earthwork cut by back lane from Gayle, Wensleydale.
             Perhaps a denuded late neolithic henge monument.

SD900794   Yockenthwaite Ring, Langstrothdale. A slightly ovoid
             arrangement of 25 boulders beside the river.
             Probably once formed a kerb around a Bronze Age
             round barrow. Some five yards to the south are three
             other rocks in a line.

SD912692	Dewbottoms. The site of a Bronze Age settlement above Cowside Beck. Clearly-defined area of enclosures and hut foundations.
SD920870	Semerwater. A glacial moraine lake in Raydale and the site of settlement almost continuously from Neolithic times. No remains.
SD949653	Druids Circle, Bordley. Three surviving upright stones of a 'Four-Poster' megalithic burial site more common in Scotland.
SD951869	Stony Raise, Addleborough, Wensleydale. A cairn that may contain a Bronze Age burial and featured in a legend of a local giant.
SD964645	Calf Hole cave, Skyrethorns. Mesolithic occupation.
SD983873	Castle Dykes, Aysgarth Moor. A henge, possibly late Neolithic/early Bronze Age. Two large stones embedded in outer banking may be remains of a stone ring.
SD990903	Almost circular stone ring on Oxclose Pasture near Carperby. Largest of its type in area and some 92ft by 78ft. All 16 stones have fallen inwards from banking.
SE009613	Elbolton Cave (Navvy Noodle Hole), Wharfedale. Important site of Neolithic occupation.
SE014654	Yarnbury Henge, sometimes called 'Woodhenge'. It is 100ft across and its eastern side shows signs of excavation. Probably late Neolithic.
SE022981	Maiden Castle, Swaledale. A large henge-like earthwork, perhaps defensive and probably Iron Age.
SE031970	Ten stones forming a ring on Harkerside Moor, Swaledale. Other earthworks nearby.
SE052363	Castlestead Ring, on Cullingworth Moor 176yds west of A629 Keighley to Halifax road. Appears like a denuded henge.
SE059500	Round Dikes, Addingham Low Moor. A very large henge associated with nearby earthworks and tumuli.

SE064631	Farncarl Circle. Ring of stones on Farncarl Hill just north of B6265 Hebden to Pately Bridge Road.
SE075445	Rivock Edge above Riddlesden, Aire Valley. Area containing profusion of cup and ring marked stones.
SE093495	Possible site of Bronze Age fortified camp occupying cliff-top position above the Wharfe at Nessfield, Wharfedale.
SE096469	The Swastika Stone, located on Woodhouse Crag above Ilkley. A composite of cup and ring carvings dating from Bronze Age. Unique in this country.
SE126451	Twelve Apostles. Bronze Age ring consisting of gritstone slabs, probably a barrow circle.
SE130460	Green Crag Slack, Burley Moor, Wharfedale. Area exhibiting Bronze Age enclosures, cairns and barrows.
SE133435	Stone ring comprising 50 stones, 260yds NE of Horncliffe Well on Hawksworth Moor.
SE137447	Stone ring on Burley Moor. Consists of 12 stones.
SE152141	Castle Hill, Almondbury. Hill top site of neolithic earthwork and Iron Age fort.
SE270800	Henge located in wood near Nosterfield.
SE285795	Thornborough Henge. A sadly-neglected monument of Neolithic age 1½ miles north east of West Tanfield. The earthwork has a diameter of 900ft and originally had bankings 10ft high.
SE288788	Henge east of West Tanfield. With above two forms a linear arrangement of earthworks.
SE392665	Devil's Arrows, Boroughbridge. Three standing stones most likely Bronze Age. The largest is 22ft high.
TA097677	The Rudstone, a 25ft-tall megalith located within the churchyard at Rudston. Britain's tallest standing stone, dating probably from Bronze Age.

Appendix Two

Tumuli and Barrows

It has been estimated that there was over 10,000 burial mounds in the North York Moors region alone. Many of these suffered the attentions of treasure seekers in the Middle Ages and later periods.

These tumuli are often referred to as *howes*, a word derived from the Old Norse for a low hill. Below is a select list of some major named sites.

The Dales

SD709787   Apron-Full of Stones. Possible Anglo-Norse burial on the east bank of Kingsdale Beck 3½ miles north of Ingleton.

SD857733   Giant's Grave, located on the edge of Penyghent fell beside the Stainforth-Halton Gill moor road. Denuded remains of Neolithic chambered grave.

SD907654   Seaty Hill on Malham Lings. A unique hill top Bronze Age burial site.

SD971569   Scale House Barrow, near Rylstone. Site of important Bronze Age burial with corpse contained in a split log.

The Wolds and North York Moors

NZ537029   Drake's Howe, adjacent to boundary stone on Cringle Moor.

NZ703008	Loose Howe. Located near West Gill Head. Excavation in 1937 revealed a Bronze Age split-log burial.
NZ766994	Wheeldale Howe. Some 200yds. N.E. of Blue-Man-in-the-Moss standing stone.
NZ842089	Swarth Howe. On north side of A171, reached by forest track opposite car park.
NZ887992	Louven Howe. Adjacent to O.S. trig. point on Stony Leas.
NZ939074	Hilda's Howe. Named after St Hilda, Abbess of Whitby Abbey.
NZ941998	Jugger Howe.
NZ944002	Jugger Howes, a pair of barrows near path across Jugger Howe Moor.
NZ957007	Stony Marl Howes. Five barrows near Ravenscar.
NZ962992	Penny Howe, located just off A171 on Harwood Dale Moor.
NZ963019	Robin Hood's Butts. Group of three mounds on Brow Moor south of Robin Hood's Bay.
NZ968001	Pie Rigg Howe, in woodland north of A171.
NZ972011	Beacon Howes, a mile west of Ravenscar, near radio mast.
SE542946	Sour Milk Hills. Two barrows on Hawnby Moor north of Low Thwaites.
SE544967	Joseph Wade's Hut. A single mound on Meggy Mire.
SE644377	Dane's Hills. A group of five tumuli in woods two miles east of Riccall.
SE739929	Abraham's Hut. A tumulus on Black Hill.
SE821919	Pillow Mounds. Two barrows east of Moors Railway near The Grange.
SE880669	Duggleby Howe. Beside B1248 near Duggleby village. Important Neolithic tumulus.

SE889987   Lilla Howe on Fylingdales Moor. A Bronze Age tumulus surmounted by Lilla Cross, supposedly marking the grave of the Saxon, Lilla.

SE892962   Low Woof Howe. Located ¾ mile south of High Woof Howe (see below).

SE909960   Breckon Howe. In forest in Langdale, adjacent to track.

SE935879   Three Tumblers. Three barrows close to junction of paths in Wykeham Forest.

SE984967   High Woof Howe. In forest at east edge of M.O.D. land on Derwent Rigg Head.

TA018633   Danes Graves. Group of three barrows in woods north of Great Kendale.

TA062724   Willy Howe, reputed haunt of goblins 1½ miles west of Burton Fleming.

TA917410   Long Barrow, a Neolithic tumulus two miles east of Market Weighton.

Appendix Three

Iron-Age Sites

This includes the more important sites of this period, both British and Roman. The latter should be viewed within the context of the Iron-Age, a period which continued for some time after the Roman withdrawal.

NY 914014   Arngill Scar. A few hut circles on terrace overlooking Kisdon Gorge.

NZ112074   Castlesteads. Earthwork on a spur overlooking Throstle Gill one mile south of Dalton. Appears to be Iron Age.

NZ181114   Toft Hill, Stanwick. A 600 acre site of defensive earthworks built by Venutios in the late 1st century to resist the Roman advance.

NZ568183   Eston Nab. Iron Age adaptation of Bronze Age hillfort site overlooking Eston village at the northern limb of the North York Moors region, overlooking Middlesborough.

NZ608116   Iron Age settlement located slightly north of Lonsdale Plantation, Kildale moor. A well-preserved site showing hut circles with paved floors and walls a few courses high.

NZ766144   Borrowby Moor, North York Moors. Iron Age enclosures.

NZ831922   Enclosure at head of Pigtrough Griff, Levisham Moor.

NZ835151   Goldsborough. Hill top site of Roman signal station one mile north of the village. Little more than a few grassy mounds now.

SD743745   Ingleborough Hill, near Ingleton. One of the most impressive hill fort sites, and the highest in Britain. Possibly the Rigodunum mentioned by Ptolemy. Enclosed within a perimeter wall (ruined) are the foundations of several hutments.

SD792802   The Roman road from Overburrow to Bainbridge, once known as the Devil's Causeway. Grid reference marks the beginning, at Axletree Gill, where the paved way climbs east to become the Pennine Way from Cam End.

SD802674   'Celtic Wall', Ribblesdale. An isolated section of dry-stone wall, 5ft thick. Attributed as Iron Age, though not substantiated. May mark the site of an important burial.

SD896638   Malhamdale. An area, several acres in extent, of enclosures dating from the Romano-British years.

SD915645   Marching camp, Mastiles Lane. Site of large Roman camp on Malham Moor. There is no obvious water supply, so probably built as an exercise by legionaries based at Elslack.

SD925495   Burwen castle, Elslack. Roman fort of Olenacum, built to secure the military road linking York with Ribchester. Ramparts and some stonework visible.

SD935849   Field system 250 yards south-west of site below.

SD937851   Enclosure with six hut circles on Stake Allotments, 250 yards west of bench mark at bend in Busk Lane. Possibly Iron Age.

SD937902   Virosidum (High Seat). Roman fort built in the Agricolan period about AD 98 on the summit of Brough Hill overlooking the village of Bainbridge, Wensleydale. Some Roman walling to be seen.

SD939536   Kirk Sink, Gargrave. Site of Romano-British villa, dating from the early 4th century. A few undulations are all that remain.

SD939782   Buckden Rake. A small section of well-preserved Roman road.

SD939833   Collection of hut circles, possibly Iron Age, located on Stake Moss.

SD940809   Small settlement of two or three huts and enclosures 50 yards east of Gilbert Lane at head of Kidstones Bank.

SD941807   Hell Gap. Site of short section of causeway on Roman road over Stake Moss.

SD942945   Oxnop Scar, Summerlodge Moor. Two enclosure each with a hut circle.

SD944809   Enclosures above Kidstones Scar, probably associated with above at 940809.

SD948779   A linear arrangement of enclosures and hut circles of probable Iron Age located on terraces flanking Buckden Beck.

SD950875   Greenber Edge, Addleborough. Another small area of enclosures with iron Age hut foundations.

SD952869   Half a mile south of above. System of enclosures and hut circles.

SD971669   Outgang Hill, Kilnsey. An enclosure 150ft long by 100ft wide containing five hut circles and a pound. At the north corner is another, smaller enclosure, and 300ft to the north-east is a small field system. Could be Iron Age.

SD982905   Ivy Scar. An area of enclosures and hut circles above Woodale, Wensleydale.

SD985653   Fort Gregory, Bastow Wood, Wharfedale. Site of small Iron Age defence of Brigantes.

SD985755   Tor Dyke, Great Whernside. A mile long Iron Age rampart bisected by road from Kettlewell to Coverdale at Scale Park.

SD990175   Blackstone Edge, Rishworth Moor. Map reference is starting point of a half-mile section of Roman road. Without doubt one of the best preserved of its kind in Britain. The road is 16ft wide and is composed of interlocking gritstones with kerbstones and a central, 3ft wide channel, possibly used for the brake poles of carts.

SE005655   High Close, Grassington. Large area of Romano-British field patterns, best seen under low sunlight from Sweet Side.

SE022981   Maiden Castle, Swaledale. A large henge-like earthwork containing what appear to be hut circles. Possibly an Iron Age adaptation of an earlier Bronze Age structure.

SE025970   Harker Hill, Swaledale. An area of small enclosures, hut circles and defensive ditches and bankings. Probably Iron Age.

SE031859   An area of enclosures containing hut circles on Burton Moor a mile east of West Burton village.

SE117479   Olicana. Roman fort established beside Wharfe where Ilkley stands today. Located on an important junction of military roads. A 15-yard section of walling can be seen behind the Manor House museum.

SE152141   Castle Hill, Almondbury. This hill-top fortress is believed to have been the stronghold of Cartimandua, queen of the Brigantes. The earthworks still to be seen are probably contemporary with later Norman defences.

SE207007   Castle Dike, Langsett. Earthwork, possibly defensive, on the flank of hill overlooking A616.

SE337375   Site of Roman villa slightly east of Waterloo Lake, Roundhay in Leeds.

SE398375   Hill fort on outskirts of Barwick-in-Elmet, containing a later Norman motte.

SE402446   Dalton Parlours. Site of Romano-British villa three miles south of Wetherby.

SE406665   Aldborough, near Boroughbridge. The Roman fortified
            town of Isurium Bragantium. Sections of the town
            wall, interval tower and corner tower visible. Also
            some fine mosaic floors, plus a museum displaying
            Roman artifacts.

SE409380   The Ridge. Western arm of Becca Banks, a two-mile
            long rampart defence which may be part of defences
            on The Rein (below).

SE438527   The Rein. Mile-and-a-half long defensive rampart
            running south-east towards Lotherton Hall. Possible
            part of defence works of Elmet.

SE446377   South Dyke. Earthwork rampart and ditch.

SE506856   Boltby Scar, Hambleton Hill. Site of probable Iron Age
            fort overlooking Greendale.

SE782900   Cawthorne camps, North York Moors. Roman camps
            and a possible fort. Well-preserved site and
            interpretation centre north of the Pickering to
            Cropton moor road.

SE803973   Wade's Causeway, Wheeldale Moor. Map reference is
            the southernmost recognisable point of a mile-long
            section of Roman road. Scheduled as a National
            monument.

SE932287   Site of Roman villa near Ellerker, adjacent to Roman
            road from Brough-on-Humber to York.

SD996663   Lea Green, Dib Scar. A small Iron-Age settlement
            consisting of a few hut circles within an outer
            enclosure.

SK 259816   Carl Wark, Hathersage Moor. A small Iron Age fort.

SK 378910   Wincobank, Sheffield. Celtic hill fort site overlooking
            the River Don. This was the most impregnable
            fortification of its kind in the region. A double
            rampart can still be discerned embracing a 2.5 acre
            enclosure.

SK 405966   Roman Ridge. Half-mile long earthwork north of
            Wingfield. Perhaps part of linear defences extending
            from fort at Wincobank.

SK 428895   Roman Ridge, north of Upper Haugh. North-eastern continuation of above.

SK 434910   Canklow Hill, Sheffield. Earthwork, possibly defensive and Celtic in origin.

TA052892   Castle Cliff, Remains of 4th century Roman beacon tower, one of the best preserved. Contained within bailey of Norman castle. Although half of the site has been lost due to cliff erosion, original stone foundations can still be seen.

Appendix Four

Runes

The first runes are believed to have been invented around about the beginning of Christianity and remained in use during the first millenium AD. The true origin is open to much conjecture, though the influence of other alphabets, Greek, Gothic and Etruscan is apparent. In the later versions Scandinavia was to enjoy a runic alphabet one third of which was based upon the Latin form.

The alphabet consisted of twenty-four phonetic symbols, each formed from a combination of upright and diagonal strokes. They were devised principally for carving on either wood or stone, hence the lack of curved characters, and seemingly were reserved for important inscriptions only. It is thought that some runic inscriptions were believed to be endowed with magical properties.

Runes were common to all the Germanic and Scandinavian cultures apart from some minor variations between Danish, Swedish-Norwegian and Old English runes. Given their widespread use, few rune stones have been discovered, even in Scandinavia, where in Norway these number less than fifty. In Britain the greatest number occur in the Isle of Man.

In Yorkshire, a few stone crosses are embellished with English runes, notably the Anglo-Saxon examples to be found in the churches at Hackness and Collingham. The 7th century comb discovered at Whitby bears a runic prayer: 'May God look on us. May Almighty God help our race'. In the parish church at Bingley too, is a font-like stone basin locally known as the Rune Stone. It has some carved markings around its circumference, though badly eroded and illegible, may originally have been an inscription in runes.

Appendix Five

Museums Containing Important Remains

Aldborough Roman Town Museum, Aldborough, Nr. Boroughbridge

British Museum, Kensington, London

Cliffe Castle Museum, Spring Gardens Lane, Keighley

Craven Museum, Town Hall, High Street, Skipton

Dales Countryside Museum, Station Yard, Hawes

Hull and East Riding Museum, High Street, Old Town, Hull

Jorvik Viking Centre, Coppergate, York

Leeds City Museum, Calverley Street, Leeds

Malton Museum, Town Hall, Market Place, Malton

Manor House Museum, Castle Yard, Ilkley

Richmondshire Museum, Ryders Wynd, Richmond

Victoria and Albert Museum, London

York Minster Foundations and Treasury, York

Yorkshire Museum, Museum Gardens, York

Appendix 6

Plotting a 6-figure Grid Reference

All modern maps produced by the Ordnance Survey are overprinted with a National Grid. Simply, this is a series of parallel lines forming squares aligned to the central meridian of the projection of Ordnance Survey mapping. For user convenience this grid system is divided into 100 kilometre squares identified by two letters, for instance SA.

These are further sub-divided into one kilometre squares, as shown on 1:25,000 Pathfinder and Outdoor Leisure series and 1:50,000 Landranger series maps by thin lines, ruled horizontally and vertically at one kilometre intervals. Each of these is represented by a number from 00 to 99, a sequence which repeats itself every 100 kilometres. It can thus be seen that it is a straightforward matter to establish the precise location of any point in the country.

As an example, using Landranger Map 101 (Scarborough and Bridlington Area) we shall plot the six-figure location of the church in Kilham village (see Fig. 23). First we establish that the village is located in the 100 kilometre square denoted by the letters TA. Grid references are always given in Eastings and Northings.

The Eastings are always read first. For instance, note the number of the vertical grid line immediately to the left of the church, in this case 06. Now imagine that the one kilometre square, the space between the vertical line to the left of the church and the one immediately to its right, is divided again into ten equal divisions. We estimate the line nearest the church to be at about division number four (i.e. four-tenths of the way along the line) and this, added to the original '06' gives an Easting of 064. Repeat the process for the Northing to give the number 644. The full National Grid reference of the Kilham church is therefore TA064644.

To plot your own position and grid reference in the field, pin-point two landmarks clearly identifiable on the map. Compass sightings are taken to each point. From these readings, subtract the differences between magnetic north and grid north. This difference and its annual variation (usually a few minutes of arc) are indicated in the margin of the map. It is then necessary to convert the figures into back bearings, by subtracting 180 if the bearing exceeds 180 degrees or adding 180 if it is less than 180 degrees. The intersection of both lines when plotted on the map represents your true ground position.

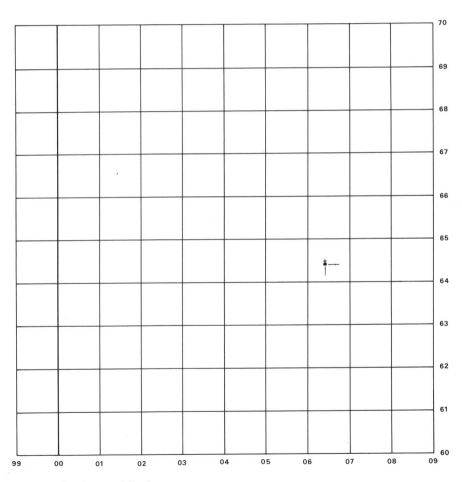

Fig. 23: Plotting a grid reference

Bibliography

Below is a select reading list for those interested enough to seek out further information on the long history of Yorkshire. Two maps are especially useful. Both were published in 1968 by the Ordnance Survey in conjunction with the York Archaeological Trust. One deals with Viking and Medieval York, the second with York as the Roman *Eboracum* and Anglian *Eoforwik*. In addition there is a map of Roman Britain, 4th edition, 1978, also published by the Ordnance Survey.

General

BLAIR, P.H. *Northumbria in the Days of Bede* (Gollancz, 1976).

CAMPBELL, J. (Ed) *The Anglo-Saxons* (Phaidon, 1982).

ELLIS, P.B. *The Celtic Empire* (Guild Publishing, 1990).

FLETCHER, R. *Who's Who in Roman Britain and Anglo-Saxon England* (Shepheard-Walwyn, 1989).

GARMONSWAY, G.N. (ed. trans.) *The Anglo-Saxon Chronicle* (Dent, 1990).

MARGARY, P.D. *Roman Roads in Britain* (London, 1973).

MORRIS, J. *The Age of Arthur* (Weidenfield & Nicolson, 1973. Reprinted 1989).

MUIR, R. *Old Yorkshire* (Michael Joseph, 1987).

PHILLIPS, G.R. *Brigantia: A Mysteriography* (Routledge & Kogan Page, 1976).

RAISTRICK, A. *Prehistoric Yorkshire* (Dalesman Pub., 1965).

RICHARDS, J.D. *Viking Age England* (BCA/Batsford, 1991).

SAWYER, P.H. *From Roman Britain to Norman England* (Methuen, 1978).

SELKIRK, R. *The Piercebridge Formula* (1983).

WOOD, M. *Domesday: A Search for the Roots of England* (BBC Publications, 1986).

Specific

BOGG, E. *From Edenvale to the Plains of York* (Goodall & Soddick, Leeds).

BOGG, E. *Wensleydale and the Lower Vale of the Yore* (Leeds).

CHILDE, V.G. *The Dawn of European Civilization* (Routledge & Kegan Paul, 1957).

ELGEE, F. *Early Man in North-East Yorkshire* (Gloucester, Bellows, 1930).

FELLOWS JENSEN, G. *Place-Names and Settlements in the North Riding of Yorkshire* (Northern Hist. 14. 1978).

GEOFFREY OF MONMOUTH (Ed. Griscom), 1929. *Historia Regum Britanniae, London.*

HARTLEY, B.R. *Roman Ilkley* (Olicana Museum & Historical Society, 1987).

HEY, D. *The Making of South Yorkshire* (Moorland Pub, 1979).

HOPE, R.C. *Holy Wells of England*, 1893.

ILKLEY ARCHAEOLOGICAL GROUP/WEST YORKSHIRE ARCHAE-OLOGICAL SERVICE *The Carved Rocks of Rombald's Moor*

JACKSON, S. *Celtic and Other Stone Heads*. (1973)

KING, A. *Early Pennine Settlement* (Dalesman, 1970).

MALORY, SIR THOMAS. *Le Morte d'Arthur* (Everyman's Library Series, London: J.M. Dent & Sons, 1941).

MORRIS, J. (Ed). *Domesday Book: Yorkshire, I & II* (Phillimore, 1986).

PHILLIPS, J. *Rivers, Mountains and Sea Coast of Yorkshire*, 1852.

RAISTRICK, A. *The Pennine Dales* (Eyre & Spottiswoode, 1968, reprinted 1969).

ROSS, A. *Pagan Celtic Britain* (Rev. Ed. Constelle, 1992).

ROSS, ANNE *The Pagan Celts* (Routledge & Kegan Paul, 1967).

SMITH, A.H. *Place-names of the North Riding of Yorkshire* (Cambridge, English Place-Name Society, 1928, reprinted 1969).

SMITH, A.H. *Place-names of the West Riding of Yorkshire* (English Place-Names Society 1961-3. 7 Vols.)

WARDELL, J. *Historical Notices of Ilkley, Rombald's Moor. Baildon Common and other Matters of the British and Roman Period, 2nd Ed.* 1881.

WHITE, S. *Standing Stones and Earthworks on the North Yorkshire Moors* (1987)

Index